GW00776975

F1 '97

KENWOOD
West
West
BOSS
BOSS
EAGLE
Mobil

West
KENWOOD
Mobil

COMPUTERVISION
Mercedes-Benz

BOSS
Mobil 1
LOCTITE
SAP
9

Shell
Shell
EUROPEAN
AVIATION

www.verstappen.nl
18
EUROPEAN
AVIATION
GOODYEAR

Ferrari Marlboro
5
Marlboro
Shell
Marlboro

photo D'Alessio

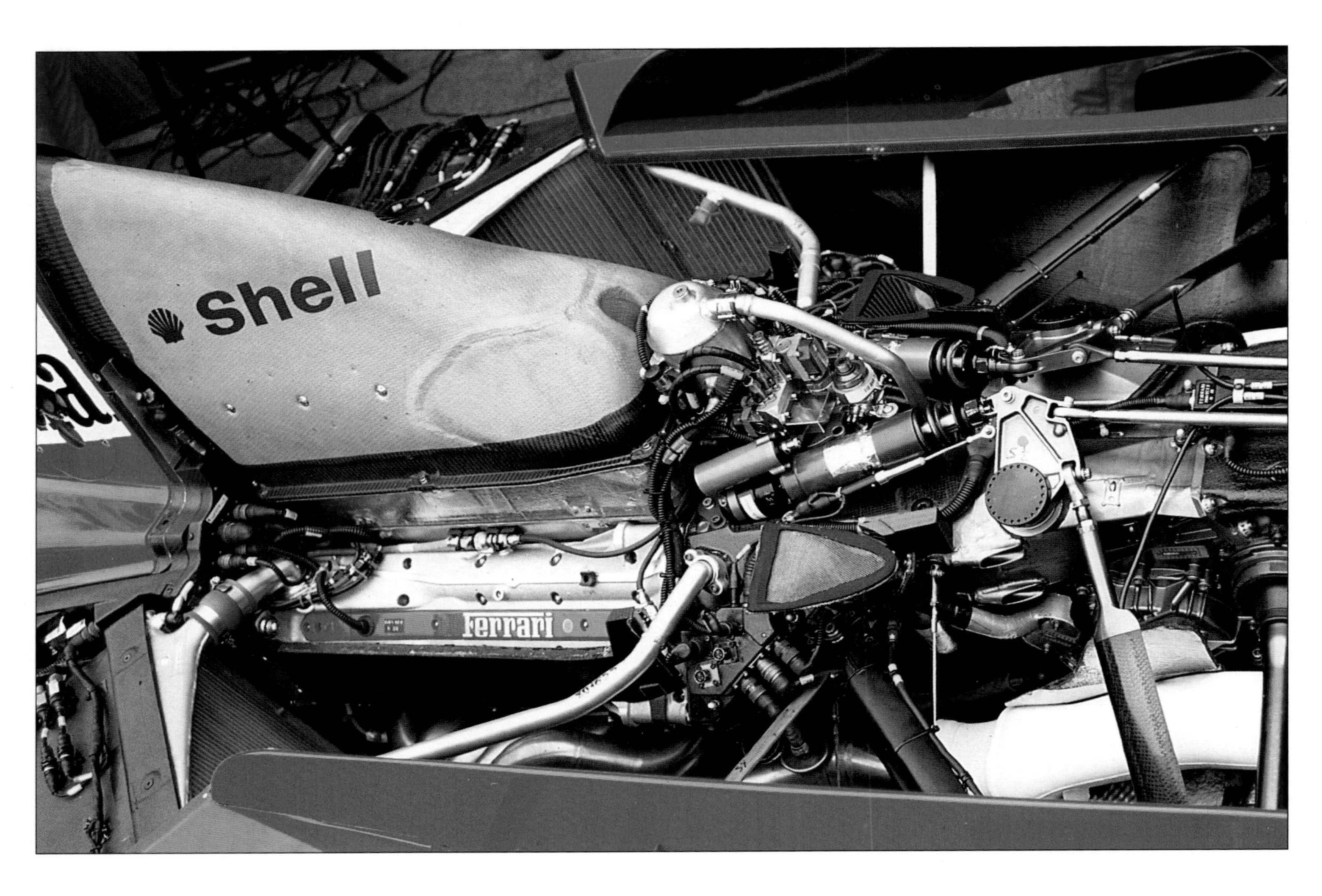
Shell
Ferrari

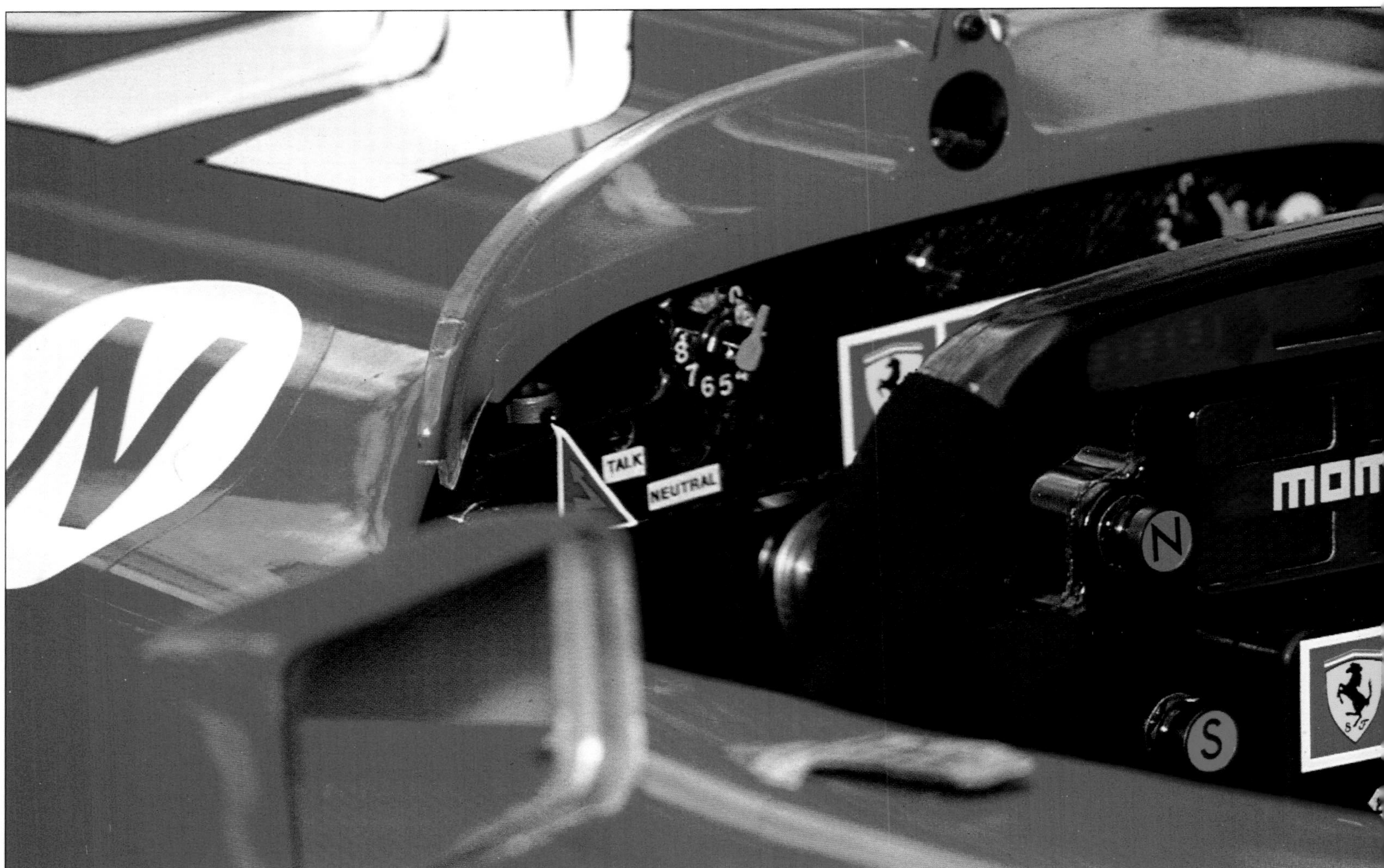
TALK
NEUTRAL

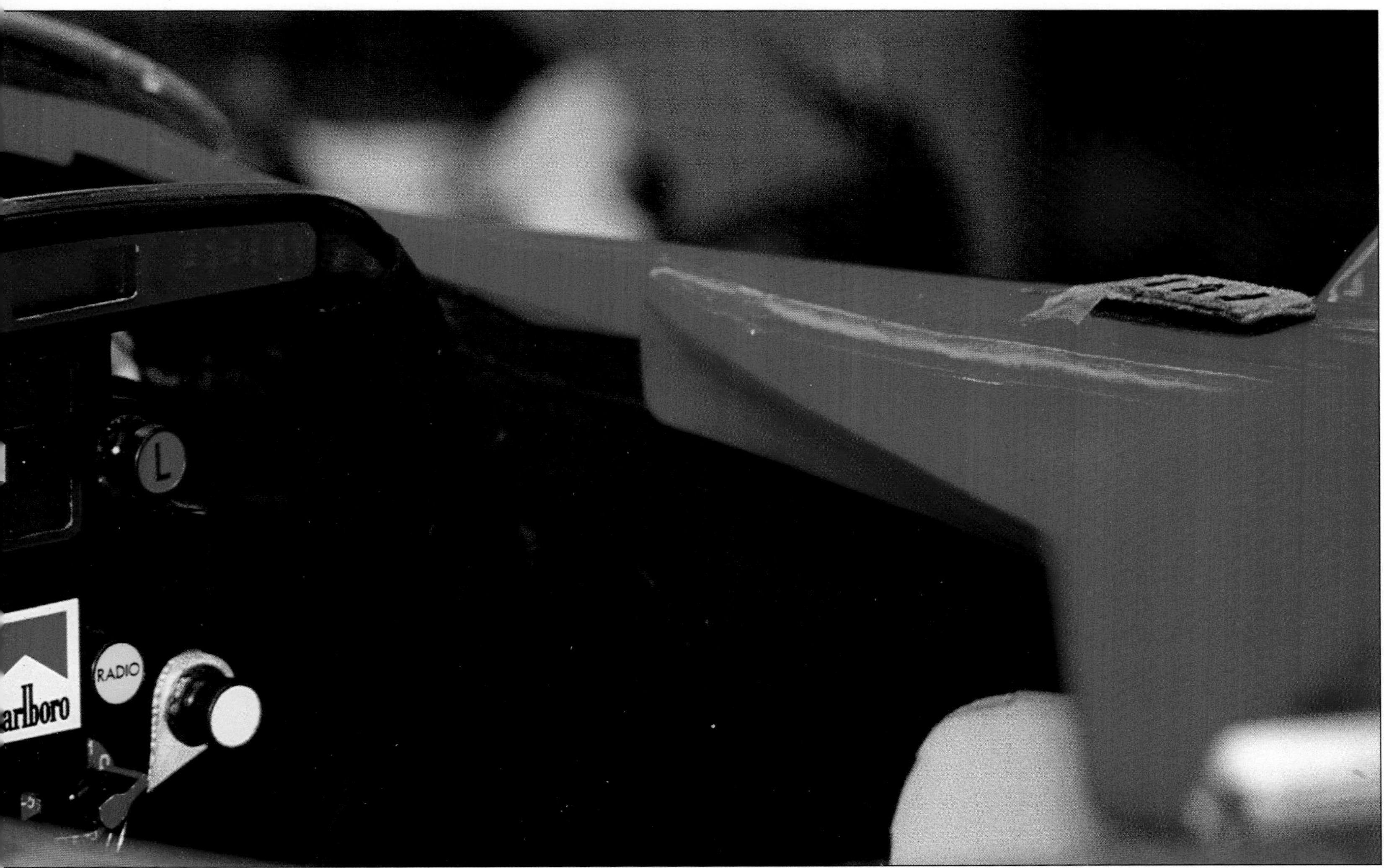

photo D'Alessio

photo D'Alessio

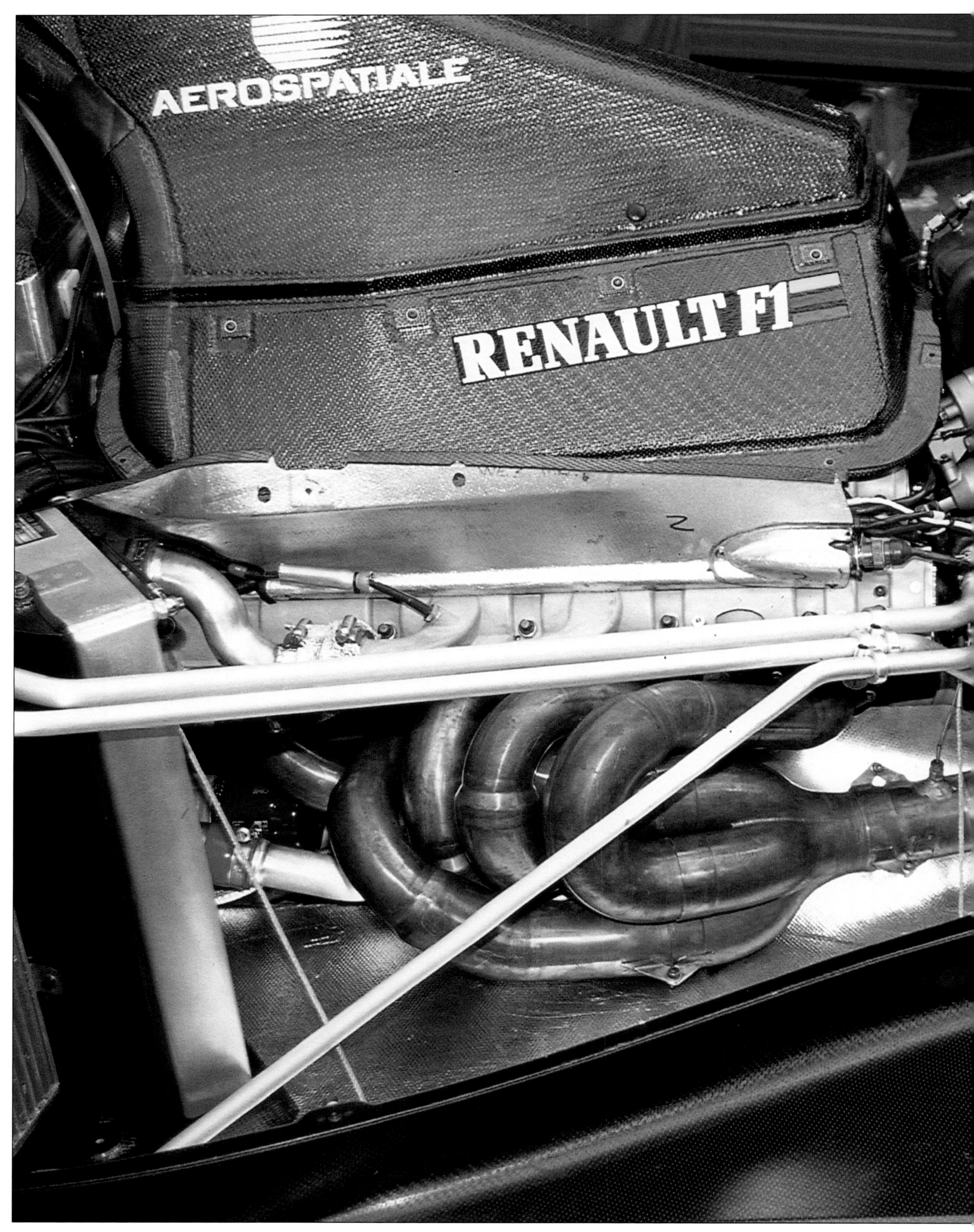
AEROSPATIALE
RENAULT F1

photo D'Alessio

photo D'Alessio

TAG HEUER
West
10
Mobil
1
BRITISH AEROSPACE
COMPUTER ASSOCIATES

PIAA
GAULOISES
GAULOISES
Marlboro
POWERHORSE

AX
LOUIS

THE RETURN OF FERRARI

The die was cast but the hand was concealed. "This year we want to win more races than in 1996 - declared the president of the Prancing Horse in January on the presentation of the new F1 car - We don't know how many more races: one, maybe two ... 1998 however will see Ferrari aiming for the world title".
Was this prudence, fear or tactics? Maybe none of these. That day, January 7th, saw the appearance of the long-awaited F310B: the first Ferrari single-seater entirely created by the genial John Barnard. The car in fact had arrived pretty soon, considering the usual lateness of the British designer.

At least four wins: one more than in 1996. This was Ferrari's aim at the start of the season. The target was reached. Michael Schumacher started winning at Montecarlo and continued throughout the summer. He catalysed around himself an increasingly competitive team which gave him a car, the F310B, which soon respected the team's ambitions, despite not being entirely perfect. And Ferrari fans everywhere began to dream ...

Marlboro
Marlboro
PIONEER
TELECOM
STET company

Marlboro
5
Asprey
PIONEER

This was due to the demands of the team, Michael Schumacher and Jean Todt above all, who knew that an adequate winter testing programme was absolutely vital if Ferrari wanted to begin the world championship with a car which was reliable, if not competitive. In fact the F310B was not exactly competitive. In the first tests against the other teams on tracks around Europe, the car did not perform well.
But at least it was reliable. At that point, the strategy throughout the season for Ferrari was clear: tests, tests and more tests.
Modifications and development would come step by step.
This was how the F310B, an 'ugly duckling' of a car, was transformed race after race into a car which was not exceptional, but atleast was reliable and whose performance improved rapidly. This was clearly due to Schumacher, but also to a team which this year, thanks to the arrival of ex-Benetton engineers Ross Brawn and Rory Byrne into the technical structure, had been strengthened and improved.

Schumacher and Irvine: Ferrari's 1997 drivers. Two different, sometimes completely different faces. The orange helmet of the Irish driver was rarely seen in the battles for the lead; often he was inexplicably half-way down the field. A long way behind the on and over-the-limit performances from his German teammate who gave Maranello and Ferrari fans everywhere the excitement of some extraordinary performances.

Marlboro
Marlboro

These were probably the missing pieces at Ferrari over the past couple of seasons, because the team had been strong but not united. The presence of a genius of a designer such as John Barnard, who had continued to work far away in England, had modified the balance within the team, and above all slowed down decision-making, design, construction and development processes.
The arrival of Brawn as technical director and Byrne as designer completed the victorious trio (the third member was Schumacher) which had taken Benetton to the 1994 and 1995 titles. Thanks to this new line-up, the Ferrari 1997 version progressed week after week without losing track of its immediate aim: obtain the best possible results on the track given the material available at the time.
The results were plain for all to see. After several years of poor, even disastrous performances, the 1997 Ferraris were reliable and consistently went well. These characteristics had been forgotten since the days of Prost and the 1990 title which he lost at the final round.

A close-up of the Ferrari F310B of Eddie Irvine. For a second successive year, the car was powered by a 10-cylinder engine: four more cylinders more than the 6-cylinder engine which in 1961 took the Ferrari 156 with Phil Hill to the conquest of the first-ever rear-engined title in the history of the Prancing Horse.

This time however, there was a plus point: Michael Schumacher, together with his perfection during qualifying and races and his almost animal-like capacity to obtain the best possible result with the means available.
That was how Ferrari began to dream again in an atmosphere which evoked the good old days. Back to the three-year period between 1975 and 1977. Back to 1979 with Scheckter, to 1982 when technical superiority was overshadowed by the tragedies of Gilles Villeneuve and Didier Pironi. The team had finally become a 'family group'.

The 1997 Ferrari year will go down in history for the legendary performances of Michael Schumacher rather than the car. The German driver, two-times world champion with Benetton in 1994 and 1995, would surely have brought a smile to the face of the founder of the Prancing Horse, Enzo Ferrari.

Marlboro
Marlboro
Marlboro
Asprey
SCHUMACHER
Marlboro
TELECOM
STET company

Henderson
Investors
Castrol
Rothmans
RACING
Rothmans

THE VILLENEUVE DILEMMA

Defining Villeneuve as a dilemma is maybe a bit excessive, but it is certain that a question-mark hangs over the head of the Canadian driver. He was fast, very fast and was not lacking in determination. These characteristics had been evident in 1996, the year when he made his debut in F1 and the year when he had chased Damon Hill towards the world title. The 1996 Williams F1 car was a cut above the rest, in fact it was almost on a different planet. Hill was not that far ahead of the opposition however and Jacques deserved much of his reputation by outclassing his teammate on a number of occasions.

In 1997 the situation was different. The Williams was unassailable at the start of the season, but as the year progressed it came down to earth. Together with its number 1

A close-up of Jacques Villeneuve, who seems to be watching the scene of his sad retirement on the first lap of the opening Grand Prix of the season in Australia.
The son of Gilles Villeneuve arrived in F1 in 1996 after success in Indycars and at the legendary Indianapolis 500 in 1995. In 1997 he confirmed his massive talent but sometimes made mistakes which gave the impression of a fragile character.

Rothmans
RENAULT
Henderson
Rothmans
http://www.icnsportsweb.com
SONAX

driver Villeneuve, who had underlined this fact during the pre-season tests, when his sole anxiety seemed to be establishing a clear hierarchy within the team over his new teammate Heinz-Harald Frentzen.

The start of the year saw Villeneuve in superb form: two victories in three races, three in the first six. The Canadian appeared to be unbeatable. Was Williams trying to convince him to follow certain technical directions? No worries: Jacques said that from now onwards, he and his chief engineer, Jock Clear would go their own way. FIA was going to bring in new regulations from 1998 onwards? He criticised them openly and was even summoned to Paris for an explanation.

The rest is recent history. Under attack from a rapidly improving Ferrari and an increasingly fast Schumacher, Villeneuve began to show signs of weakness. In addition to the rain-soaked Montecarlo

Jacques Villeneuve is a fast and attacking driver and in the second half of the season he also showed himself to be a 'calculator' He won several races (at Silverstone, Budapest, in Austria, at the Nurburgring ...) thanks to mechanical failures of those in front of him. If his luck is ignored, the 26 year-old Canadian clearly demonstrated that he had become a great champion.

RENAULT
3
HYPE
Rothmans
Rothmans

race, where the crazy decision to start on slicks was entirely the team's fault, Jacques threw away an almost certain victory in Canada when he went off at the end of the second lap. In France, 'Schummy' and his Ferrari were uncatchable and the Canadian almost threw away vital points when he went off again three laps from the chequered flag. He had a lucky victory at Silverstone thanks to the retirement of the Ferraris and Hakkinen, and in Germany he went off after a duel with Trulli in the Prost. Despite having a Williams which was universally recognised as being the best car in F1, Villeneuve was finding it hard to maintain his usual standard. Meanwhile Ferrari and Schumacher were forging ahead ...

Interlagos, 30th March, the second round of the championship. On the top of the podium of the Brazilian GP, Villeneuve celebrated his first victory of 1997, his fifth overall since his arrival in F1. That day, Jacques took the lead of the F1 championship for the first time (together with Coulthard). Afterwards, he proved he could maintain that difficult position ...

NEW FACES IN F1

1997 saw the arrival of several new faces in F1. Usually new faces in the Circus come from all continents and all latitudes with a briefcase full of dollars. But not always. Financial backing opened the doors to Vincenzo Sospiri and Riccardo Rosset, whose F1 careers were cut short with the premature end of Lola (before the second race!) without being reimbursed for the first large instalment which they had already paid to the team. In a certain sense, financial motives were behind the choice of Ralf Schumacher. Jordan opened the doors to Michael's younger brother not in exchange for immediate cash, but for the name and

New faces in F1.
One of them was Ralf Schumacher: a famous surname, less than 22 years of age when he made his debut in F1, which he reached thanks to the support of his more famous brother Michael. Schumacher Jr. made the podium at his third race, in Argentina.
There were a few doubts about his aggressive nature on the track, as was demonstrated further on in the season.
Another brilliant deb was Jarno Trulli. Twenty-three years old on the day of the British GP, the driver from Pescara started off with Minardi and then half-way through June was drafted in by Alain Prost as a replacement for the injured Olivier Panis.

KD
KD
MUGEN
HONDA
MUGEN
HONDA
giordana

HSBC
Havoline
BOSS
CALTEX
VISIT
MALAYSIA

the potential interested sponsors with which the 22 year-old German was surrounded.
Two other 'debs' arrived in different circumstances: Shinji Nakano from Osaka, Japan and Jarno Trulli from Pescara, Italy. In the case of the tiny Japanese driver with a boyish face, it was Honda which decided. The Japanese manufacturer, through the Mugen brandname, was the technical and financial backer of the entire Prost (ex-Ligier) operation. Nakano's position was therefore untouchable throughout the season. In July in fact, the team of the four-times world champion had the possibility of signing Damon Hill who was fed up with Arrows, but Mugen said that it would have suspended the supply of its powerful 10 cylinder engine if Prost had signed Hill. The situation regarding Trulli was not so complicated. The 23 year-old was young and talented and had demonstrated this in the German F3 championship.

Jan Magnussen was almost a deb but not quite. The 24 year-old Dane started off in F1 in 1995, scoring a tenth place at the Asia-Pacific GP in Japan with McLaren. But it was only this year that he did the whole season with the brand-new Stewart car. With three rounds left, he was confirmed alongside Barrichello for the 1998 season.

TOTAL
BENSON & HEDGES
GOOD YEAR
B&H
BENSON & HEDGES
PEUGEOT
s.Oliver
BENSON & HEDGES
PEUGEOT
Diavia

BENSON & HEDGES
T.E
sparco

BENSON & HEDGES
BENSON & HEDGES
Diavia

He finished under the wing of talent scout Flavio Briatore. When the latter entered the Minardi team, Trulli found a place driving for the Italian team. His first seven races at circuits he had never seen before (except for Imola) produced some positive results and he moved to Prost as a replacement for the injured Panis starting from the French GP.

The talent of these new arrivals had a sparkling effect on the 1997 F1 circus. Ralf Schumacher's exuberance behind the wheel of the Peugeot-engined Jordan and his insufferance every time he was beaten by teammate Fisichella were some of the most exciting moments of the season.

Jordan was undoubtedly the newest team of the season for its drivers. As well as Schumacher Jr., the team run by Eddie Jordan tackled its seventh season in F1 with Giancarlo Fisichella. 24 years of age, the Rome driver started off his season carefully but he soon became one of the stars of the Circus. This was also one of the reasons why Benetton wanted him at all costs for the 1998 world championship.

MILD
SEVEN
MILD
SEVEN
RENAULT
KicKers

Sometimes the excitement became too much and went over the limit, such as when he clashed with Fisichella during the Argentinian race or when he overtook Herbert and then sent his Sauber flying at Monza. Ralf Schumacher's nervousness was one of the high points of the season, but so were Trulli's convincing performances. He came to Minardi without virtually having the chance to try a F1 car and showed clear ideas and strong nerves right from the first race. Regularly faster than his teammate Katayama, Jarno earned a call from Prost exclusively due to his results. The four-times world champion had preferred him to any other candidate. Once he arrived in the French team, Trulli had difficulty living up to the previous performances of Panis, injured in Canada but the real point of reference for the team, and who returned before the end of the season.

Third in his third GP, just like Ralf Schumacher. At the British GP, Alexander Wurz scored this exceptional result in the Benetton, as a three-race replacement for the convalescent Gerhard Berger. A mountain-bike and karting champion with a technical education, the tall young Austrian (1m91cms!) was confirmed for '98 by Benetton, who will enter him alongside Fisichella.

GAULOISES
GAULOISES
Blondes
CANAL+
giordana
BRIDGESTONE
CANAL+
giordana
BRIDGESTONE

In any case Trulli had a marvellous year and his future in the F1 circus seems assured. Italy had found another top-level F1 representative. The number 1 amongst the new faces in 1997 was without a shadow of doubt Giancarlo Fisichella. He was not a 'deb' in the strict sense of the word. But seeing as in 1996 he was unable to do much with the Minardi, his arrival in the

Trulli (large photo, above) and Nakano (see box): the two Prost drivers were 49 years old in total ... Twenty-seven years of age for Pedro Paulo Diniz, who finished his third full season in 1997 as the often fast teammate of Damon Hill at Arrows, which confirmed him for '98.

Safra

very fast Peugeot-engined Jordan F1 can be considered a debut in the top ranks of F1. Always fast, very decisive, prone to errors, Giancarlo did more than just amaze. He impressed everyone, not just the fans; even Eddie Jordan himself, who never gave up on the idea of losing him for the coming season to Benetton, after receiving him on loan in 1997 from the Italian team. Even famous drivers such as Lauda and Berger spoke well of Fisichella. Even Michael Schumacher, who despite a word for the performances of brother Ralf, said many times that he was impressed by the abilities of the young driver from Rome. Fisichella's greatest merit was that he managed to keep his head above water and replied exclusively with his performances on the track to the pressure which suddenly comes with arrival in the top echelons of the sport.

New faces ... but not for long. That was the destiny of Italy Vincenzo Sospiri and Brazilian Ricardo Rosset: the former made his debut in F1, the latter had finished a full year with Arrows in 1996. Different experiences, identical destiny: at the second round of the 1997 championship in Brazil, they found out that Lola had pulled out of F1, leaving them without a drive.

PROST AND STEWART: THE RETURN OF THE CHAMPIONS

Together, they make up an impressive array of trophies: 7 world title, 78 victories, 50 pole positions, 56 fastest laps. We're talking about Jackie Stewart and Alain Prost, idols of F1 as drivers respectively in the 1970s and 1980s, and now back on the scene as constructors. Jackie's and Alain's debuts as team managers are full of significance and worthy of detailed analysis, because they are similar in many ways but different in many others. For some time, the circus had known about the debut of Stewart Racing in F1. At least since the days when the three times world champion (1969, '71 and '73, for all those with short memories) had

Hands always moving, confirming his innermost thoughts. Always attentive, a man who centres everything around himself and who concentrates on every little detail: Alain Prost returned to F1 in 1997 as a constructor, but he wasn't much different to the driver who left it at the end of 1993 (after winning his fourth title). Return to the scene also for Jackie Stewart, here with the tartan cap of his family and together with Damon Hill. The brand-new Stewart team scored a second place with Barrichello at Montecarlo, its fifth GP of the season.

Ford
Havoline
STEWART
PELTOR
STEWART
FIA FORMULA 1 WORLD CHAMPIONSHIP
VISIT

set up a Formula 3000 team for his son, Paul, who had been a good but not exceptional driver in that category. It was clear that the team's aim was F1. This aim was realized at the start of 1997, and was the conclusion of many years of planning activity which included a search for sponsorship as well as work on the technical front. Just as he did when he was racing, Jackie Stewart left nothing to chance in the creation of his family team. He managed to obtain a supply of the 10 cylinder Ford engines in exclusive. He was able to lure Alan Jenkins away from Arrows and sign Barrichello as one of the drivers at the start of 1996. He even managed to give rise to a new Scottish tartan called Stewart Racing, which was officially registered and which was a combination of two which already existed in the names of himself and his son Paul.

Once the championship got underway, Stewart F1 continued exactly along the same path: maxi-

The logo - and the power - of Honda on the nosecone of the Prost. From 1998 onwards, the cars of the four-times world champion will be powered by the 10 cylinder Peugeot engine and the V10 Mugen-Honda will move to Jordan.
The Stewart nosecone is dominated by the Ford logo. It will be the same in 1998, the second season for the Scottish team founded by the three times world champion (1969, '71 and '73) Jackie and run by his son and former driver, Paul.

FOSTER'S
PREMIO
FORMULA
WORLD
CHAMPIONSHIP
1993
ENAULT
elf
LONGINES
MAGNETI MARELLI
MICHELIN

mum planning, no high hopes, and no giving in when faced with problems. The Ford V10 continually suffered engine failures? "It'll go better next year". Constant mechanical failures? "No problem, we're making progress". The first important result, helped by the rain but in any case one which did not come by chance, was Barrichello's second place at the Monaco GP. At the end of the race, the sight of Jackie and his son Paul congratulate one another soaked with rain brought a moment of humanity to Formula 1.

The creation of the Prost Grand Prix Team was slightly different. In this case, the interest of the four-times world champion (1985, '86, '89 and '93, again for those with even shorter memories) in the almost defunct Ligier team had also been known for some time. But Alain's decision to become a constructor was quite a surprise.

Seven world titles in 25 seasons. In 1983 (large photo on opposite page), Prost was on the point of winning the world championship; he eventually managed it in 1985, '86 and '89 with the McLaren-Honda. His fourth title came in 1993 with teh Williams-Renault, a year when he scored seven wins, including one at Imola. The three titles won by Jackie Stewart came in 1969, '71 and '73. He won a total of 27 Grand Prixs including three at Montecarlo.

STEWART
GRAND PRIX
Ford
Havoline
BRIDGESTONE
Ford
Ford
TEXACO
Havoline
BRIDGESTONE

With a short and succinct press release, like all releases, the F1 world was aware of the change. It must be underlined however that the capital for this new venture came from Prost alone. Afterwards the ex-world champion managed to exploit his characteristics as a man of prestige by guarenteeing the support of partners such as the French TV station Canal+, the tobacco company Seita, but above all the support of Peugeot which would supply its exceptional V10 engines in exclusive to the team until the end of the century.
Once his former enemy Cesare Fiorio (at their time in Ferrari) and Olivier Panis had been confirmed as sporting director and leading driver, Alain set about attacking the F1 world. He did this with total personal commitment, exactly like the way he drove. He did it with one eye on the future and with the satisfaction of results which were at times incredible.
It is all thanks therefore to Jackie Stewart and Alain Prost that the F1 of the future, which is now increasingly tied to appearance and sponsors more than late braking manoevres, has rediscovered its links with an unforgettable past.

Alain Prost with Cesare Fiorio: the 1990 driver-team manager line-up for Ferrari got back together again at Prost Grand Prix, but this time the Frenchman was in charge.
Family gathering with a common theme: a Rolex Daytona cronograph on the wrist of Jackie Stewart, his son Paul and Barrichello. The Brazilian driver admired the watch on Jackie's wrist, and his team owner promised him one the first time he qualified in the top ten. Rubens managed this feat at the third round in Argentina (5th fastest time on the third row alongside Ralf Schumacher's Jordan) and the promise was maintained.

Damon Hill's worried look.
After his 1996 triumphs with Williams, the British champion did not have a very good year with the Yamaha-powered Arrows.
Not only was he unable to challenge for the championship, but he also failed to add to his 21 GP victories.

DANKA
FERRETTI
FERRETTI
DANKA
zepter
INTERNATIONAL
parmalat
DANKA
zepter
1
zepter
zepter
POWER
HORSE
ENERGY-DRINK
POWER
HORSE
ENERGY-DRINK

DAMON HILL: MISSING IN ACTION

The disappointment could be seen in his eyes at certain points of the season. Disappointment over the fact that he suddenly found himself on the final few rows of the grid. Disappointment over the fact that he had finished another GP before the chequered flag, when something broke on his car without him being able to fight for a top 6 position.

Damon Hill's 1997 soon turned into a nightmare. After leaving the Williams team which a few months before had taken him to the world title, the British driver soon found himself having to get to grips with an Arrows-Yamaha which clearly showed its limitations ... on a performance and reliability level. His retirement from the first race in Australia during the positioning lap was memorable. But many other times, despite the technical

A difficult season for Hill, especially in the first few races. His number 1 Arrows was rarely competitive and often unreliable. The start of the 1997 season for the world champion was an uphill struggle, but improved slightly following the arrival in the team of John Barnard as technical director. Although Hill's steering-wheel was the height of technology, just like the others, the results failed to come just the same.

DANKA
POWER
HORSE
YAMAHA

POWER
HORSE
MOËT

DANKA
zepter

revolution within the team which lead to the sacking of Frank Dernie, replaced by the Genius, John Barnard who had been released by Ferrari, Damon Hill's efforts almost brought a tear to the eye of British fans and F1 followers in general.
"Having to race in this way is difficult: it is hard to find the stimulus to push hard". That was Damon's answer half-way through the season as he tried to hurry from the pit-garage to the motorhome in a not entirely successful attempt to escape the media. Half-way through July, at the British GP, came the final lament. "For next year, I want a new team and a ten million dollar contract: I know I'm worth it". This was the headline in the British newspapers - but how faithfully it respects the declarations of the driver is a different story. During qualifying for the race, Damon was slower than his less expert teammate Diniz, who had managed to

On the track with the Arrows A18, in the pits talking via radio with team owner Tom Walkinshaw. Hill had a difficult season and his 1996 title victory was soon forgotten. There was only one flash of genius: the Hungarian GP, which he dominated until a few kilometres from the chequered flag before gearbox problems put paid to hopes of victory. But a podium place alongside winner Villeneuve and the massive Hungarian trophy brought a smile to Hill's face.

LOCTITE
KENWOOD
Mobil 1
Mercedes-Benz
West

repeat this result a number of other times during the season. At Silverstone, not far from headquarters, the team reprimanded Hill, accusing him of poor performances and of not concentrating on the job in hand, thus feeding the controversy.

In 1997 Damon experienced very few positive moments. One of them however will never be forgotten: mid-August in Hungary, second row of the grid, almost certain victory until an absurd gearbox seizure on his Arrows gave him second place behind Villeneuve's Williams ... the Williams which had been his just one year before.

At the end of the day, F1 tends to forget quickly. That's how Damon soon found that one of his few convinced followers was Eddie Jordan, who wanted him at the wheel of one of his cars for the 1998 season. But the 1996 title is a long way away. And the story continues ...

Mika Hakkinen was fast on the track. David Coulthard, who won the first GP of the season in Australia, signing autographs in the pits. In 1997 these two drove an increasingly competitive but still slightly unreliable McLaren. In 1998 they know they have the right car for the championship race.

McLAREN-MERCEDES: THE RETURN OF THE SILVER ARROWS

At the start of the season, it was clear that McLaren could not afford to wait another year before returning to the top of the podium. Three years without a win were just too long. Few memories remain of the 1993 Australian GP, the fifth won that year by Senna against Williams superiority and in fact the Brazilian moved to the team the following year. After just one season ('94) with Peugeot (not necessarily the fault of the French manufacturer), the second most successful constructor in F1 after Ferrari began its third season with Mercedes in 1997. Neither the Stuttgart giant nor the British team had any intention of completing a new season without being on the top rung of the podium. This objective was reached ... at the first round. Although victory in Australia came about due to the problems of the others rather

Winner of the first round in Australia, David Coulthard scored his second victory of the year with the number 10 McLaren at Monza. While his teammate was winning, Mika Hakkinen was thinking about the future. He managed to focus his concentration despite mechanical failures which cost him at least two victories: at Silverstone and at the Nurburgring, where he set the first pole position of his career.

Mobil 1
Mercedes-Benz

West
KENWOOD
Mobil

than the technical merits of the McLaren-Mercedes, the Anglo-German combination has shown its muscles on a number of other occasions throughout the year. At round 6 in Spain, the debut of the German 10-cylinder 'evolution' engine guarenteed a power boost and bottom-end performance which helped Hakkinen and Coulthard to really fly. This progress was in part compromised by the increased fragility of the engine with respect to the previous version. It was mechanical failure in fact which cost Hakkinen his first-ever F1 victory and the second for the team at the British GP. Despite a question-mark which still hangs over engine reliability, it is clear that the leap in quality of Ron Dennis' F1 car is linked inextricably with Mercedes.
Moreover, that is the way it should be. The decision at the end of 1994, when the agreement between McLaren and Peugeot was broken in order to switch to Mercedes, clearly demonstrated how much Ron Dennis held in consideration a partnership with the Germans for the best future of his team.
On the other hand, the Stuttgart manufacturer was committed right from the start with long-term plans

*Hakkinen and Coulthard in action.
The Finn was often the faster of the two, but the Scottish driver guarenteed more constant performances for McLaren and the famous Mercedes three-pointed star.*

KENWOOD
10

aiming to revive the era of the Silver Arrows and their domination of the category in the early 1950s. 1997 saw the result of all these policies: the cars were more competitive, the engines were the most powerful and the team had finally emerged from a technical and design status quo thanks to the signing of Adrian Newey. This has come about with increasing influence from the German manufacturer, so much so that it has been officially announced that starting from the year 2000 the team will be called Mercedes, and no longer McLaren, just as in the same year the Williams will be called a BMW-Williams. Mercedes has returned in a big way therefore ... and not just because the V10-engined McLarens have become the third force in the battle between Williams and Ferrari for the title. The growing involvement of the German manufacturer goes beyond that: it is taking F1 back into the hands of the major car manufacturers, as it was 40 years ago. That is why we can now say that the Silver Arrows are back ... and are here to stay.

From half-way through the season onwards, thanks to the arrival of the ex-Williams designer Adrian Newy as technical director, the McLaren MP4/12 showed excellent progress, with top-level performance. Now that the reliability problems of the V10 Mercedes have been resolved and Coulthard and Hakkinen confirmed, the 1998 season for the silver cars promising to be a superb one.

momo
N
L
S
RADIO
MIX
EBC
DIFF

76°C
0
OIL/P OIL/T AIR/P WATER
ALARMS
NEU
GB
SPEED
personal

SPACE-AGE TECHNOLOGY

The revolution came at the end of 1988, when a genius called John Barnard proposed the first example of a semi-automatic gearbox to Ferrari for the 1989 world championship. Extremely rapid gear changes were the main characteristics of this innovation. But the revolution came from the fact that the traditional gear-lever was eliminated: in its place were two levers located behind the steering-wheel. This allowed the driver to change gear without taking his hands off the steering-wheel. Now this type of gear change is used by all the most important F1 teams, and technology has made giant strides in this sector since then.

Space-age technology, in the true sense of the word. For materials and applied technology, F1 cars are increasingly turning to aviation companies.
The steering-wheels, which are brimming with buttons and controls, reflect the massive growth in technology in Grand Prixs. Other page above, clockwise: the steering-wheels with electro-hydraulic gearbox controls of the Prost, McLaren and Stewart cars. The fourth and final steering-wheel is the most advanced: the one on the Ferrari F310B which also has a mini data monitor.

FIA
BOSS
GOODYEAR
TAG HEUER

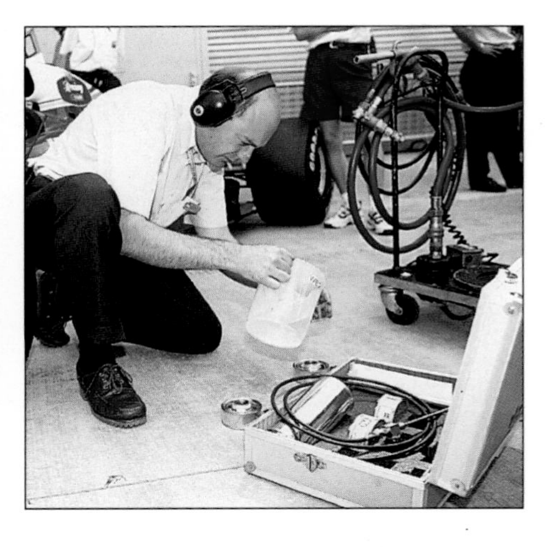

Jacques Villeneuve's Williams as a steering-wheel with a balance-lever connected to the gearbox. If he presses it, he can change upwards; pulling it towards him, he changes down. On the left of the steering-wheel, the Canadian has a manual command which disconnects the clutch during the start: this is used on all F1 cars which now have only brake and accelerator pedals.

But steering-wheel technology has progressed even further. The amount of buttons and switches have increased on the steering

The regulations limiting fuel composition are some of the strictest norms in F1. Fuel checks are frequent and random. Williams had this experience during the year (above and below the FIA inspector taking a fuel sample) and so did McLaren, alongside. Cooling of the fuel is totally banned, because it increases performance.

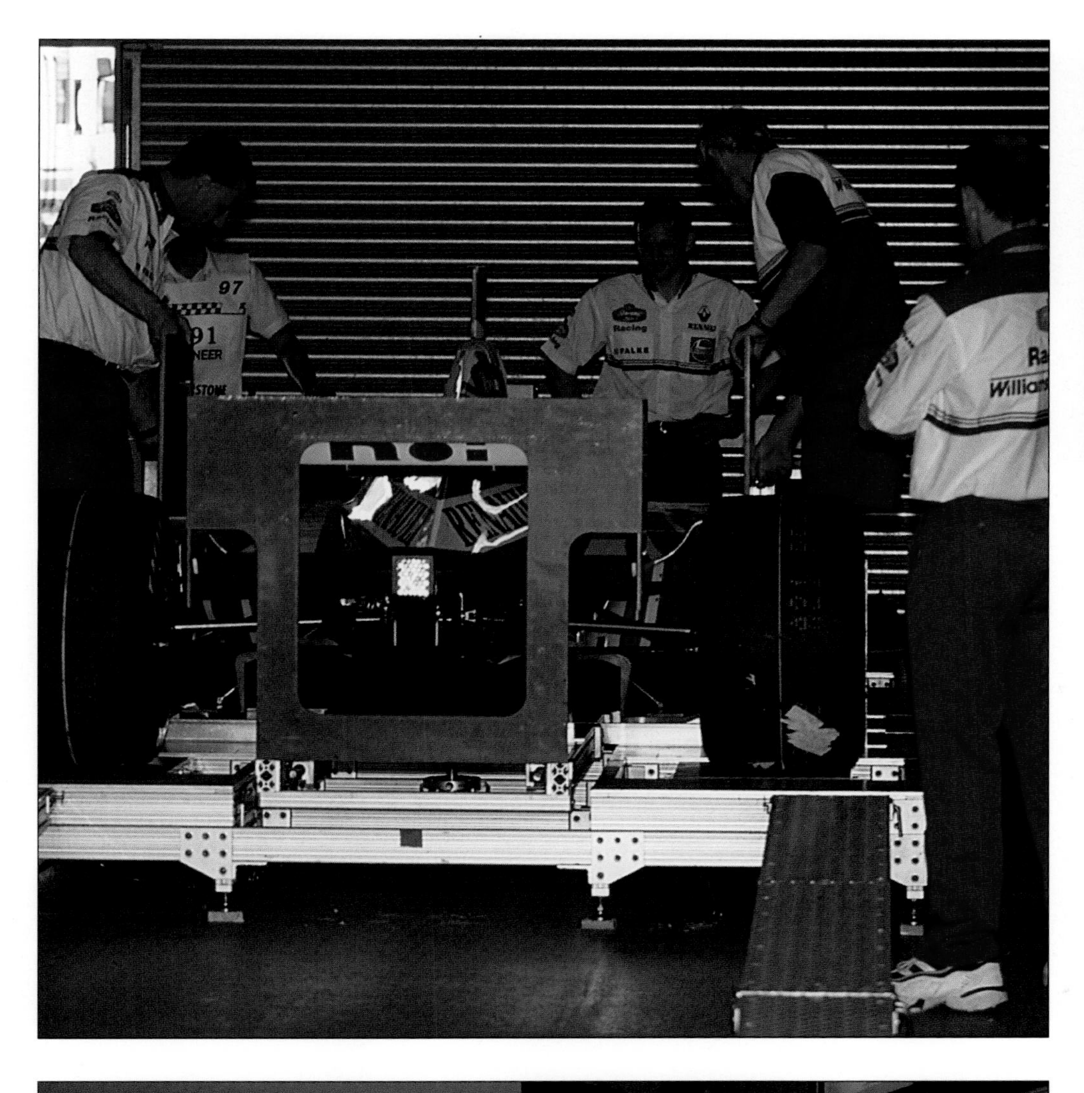

wheel and allow the driver to switch on and off several different mechanisms with a finger: from the variation of the air-fuel mixture for the cylinders, to the electronic regulation of the differential, and radio communication with the pits. Thanks to Barnard's innovation however, it was Ferrari which presented the first multi-function steering-wheel; a sort of display unit visible between the hands of the driver, which as well as giving him the possibility of controlling various mechanisms without taking his hands off the wheel, means he can control data on the monitor regarding speed, engine revs as well as lap time.

But the technology race in Formula 1 is not only confined to the driver cockpit. Electronics dominate behind the scenes in the secret team working areas, where dozens of giant monitors and computers receive data on every aspect of a F1 car. From the engine to the gearbox; but also partial time and analysis in each curve; data on tyre and brake temperatures; lateral acceleration and conti-

Headphones, headphones and more headphones. Life in the pits revolves around safe and private radio communications. Data-monitoring is today a constant factor for all teams in F1, the pit garages of which are full of computers and everything else necessary for analysing the way the car behaves on the track. In the face of this ultra-modern technology, the checks made on the car dimensions seem totally out of date.

TAG
HEUER
a timing and computing

nually variable aerodynamic downforce. Today there are no details about the lap which the driver has just completed which are concealed from computers ... not even the little white lies the drivers sometimes tell!

Away with hand-held timing: today's GP time-keeping is a science down to the thousandth of a second. Each time, before it appears on the monitor, is transmitted by a microchip on each car. Jump starts can no longer be seen with the naked eye: this is the job of a sensor placed in the tarmac on each starting-grid position.

TAG HEUER
Diavia
B&H
BENSON & HEDGES
& HEDGES
s.Oliver

THE OTHER TEAMS

Formula 1 had not produced such a star-filled season for a long time. With the years of Williams monopoly over, the 1997 edition of the Circus produced qualifying sessions and races where the gap between the top drivers was finally minimal, giving days of glory - even without a victory - to many others. The review of the other teams in the 1997 championship cannot fail to start with Benetton. The Anglo-Italian team was on a downward slide, starting with the results of 1996 (with no victories) which coincided with the departure of Michael Schumacher for Ferrari. After the loss of Rory Byrne and Ross Brawn (both headed for Ferrari), Benetton found itself in a major identity crisis. Despite this, the 1997 car immediately demonstrated its fundamental validity. A U-turn in the electronics sector - too complicated at the start of the season - was all that was necessary to restore competitivity to the B197, as the victory of Berger in Germany confirmed in July, after a series of placements and points for Alesi. But the question-mark which surrounds Benetton has for a long time revolved around the future destiny of Flavio Briatore, the man who created the miraculous multicoloured car out of nothing. Once the end of the partnership with the manager from Piedmont had been confirmed for the end of the

In its six-year F1 existence, Jordan had never come as close to victory as in 1997. Above all thanks to Giancarlo Fisichella, who after eight GPs with Minardi in 1996, moved to the cockpit of the ultra-fast Peugeot-engined Jordan 197. In Belgium, the Italian finished second behind Schumacher's Ferrari.

PAGES 76-77
Fischella was hoping for a victory at Monza after qualifying third, just 76/1000ths of a second behind Alesi on pole with the Benetton. Giancarlo finished the Italian GP in fourth place, less than 6 seconds behind winner Coulthard.

6065

B&H
BENSON & HEDGES
TOTAL

season, Benetton was able to, and had to, reorganize itself. The younger of the Benetton brothers, Rocco entered the team management, and the support of a British structure was found for the technical management of the team and the cars. Briatore's driver strategies were also changed: away with the 'old' and costly champions such as Berger and Alesi, and in with new stars such as Fisichella, who was finally prised away from the team which he had raced for in 1997, Jordan.

This review of the other teams in F1 continues with Jordan. The Irish team manager continued the path he had always followed: great attention to sponsors and marketing, commercial strategies and advertising. But as the team was finally in possession of a competi-

Benetton's season was an uphill struggle. Jean Alesi had victory in hand for half of the Italian GP, but in the other races he was usually to be found with this expression on his face. Especially after 'parking' his B197 at Magny-Cours close to these similar-coloured tyres ...

PAGES 80-81
A disappointing championship for Tyrrell as well, with the 025 car which was powered by the 8 cylinder Ford Cosworth Ed4. On slow, twisty circuits such as here at Montecarlo, the Tyrrell sprouted side-wings alongside the cockpit.

BENETTON
RENAULT
RENAULT
BENETTON POWER BY RENAULT

PIAA
EUROPEAN
EPSON

2
DANKA
DANKA
DANKA

POWER BY
YAMAHA
DANKA
DANKA

sparco
GOOD YEAR
RACING TEAM

titve car, the 197, powered by a super engine such as the 10 cylinder Peugeot and with two fast young drivers of the calibre of Fisichella and Ralf Schumacher, Jordan surprisingly found itself up there at the top. This trend will almost certainly continue in the future. After losing Peugeot (which in 1998 will race exclusively with Prost Racing), the British team has pulled off a major coup by obtaining the 10 cylinder Mugen-Honda. This unit however is becoming increasingly less Mugen and more Honda, which promises well for the future. Japanese engines instead were the bane of the Arrows team, which started at full gas at the beginning of the season and which became less and less competitive race after race. The slide was halted by the arrival of John Barnard. Penalized by the disappointing V10 Yamaha, the Arrows struggled throughout the year, forcing its star driver Damon Hill to look for another drive with Jordan.

Propping up this list as well as the championship table are Tyrrell and Minardi. The British team suffered throughout 1997, but at the end of the season had a smile on its face with the signing of a contract which from 1998 onwards will guarante the team the Ford V10 engine in its customer version. Above all this brought an end to the rumours that the team was up for sale, and a new wind tunnel and future strategies are some sort of guaranteee for the future. New strategies also for Minardi in 1997 and next year, which give it a financially sound future and hopefully some important results.

PAGES 82-83
The 10 cylinder Yamaha engine was one of the weak points of the Arrows A18: a car from the pen of designer Frank Dernie which was improved race by race by new technical director John Barnard.

PAGES 84-85
A second season in Benetton did not enable Jean Alesi to repeat his only F1 victory, in the 1995 Canadian GP with Ferrari. The French driver of Italian origin concluded the 1997 season with 134 Grand Prixs disputed since his debut in 1989 with Tyrrell.

Ferrari
RENAULT
RENAULT
BRIDGESTONE
Marlboro
Marlboro
Marlboro
Marlboro
BRIDGESTONE
BRIDGESTONE
BRIDGESTONE
BRIDGESTONE

PAGES 86-87
A splendid panoramic view of one of the most difficult and fascinating circuits left in F1: Interlagos, on the outskirts of the Brazilian megalopolis of San Paolo. Schumacher's Ferrari, in second, leads the Benetton of Berger, who might have been able to challenge Villeneuve for victory, had he not been held up at that point of the circuit for a number of laps.

Pages 88-89
A wheel-smoking Ralf Schumacher brakes in Hungary; it was his fifth finish in the points and third successive fifth position. After the race, the 22 year-old German driver of the Jordan was criticised for not having caused problems to his brother Michael, who was fourth just 214 thousandths of a second ahead of him and easy pickings due to the suspension problems of his Ferrari.

Pages 90-91
On the podium in his third race, in Argentina, Ralf Schumacher is the most controversial of all the brothers involved in F1 Grand Prixs. A quick mention for the others: Pedro and Ricardo Rodriguez, Emerson and Wilson Fittipaldi, Jody and Ian Scheckter, Teo and Corrado Fabi, Manfred and Joachim Winkelhock.

Pages 92-93
Top-level technology: brakes. During the 1997 world championship season, 38 mm brake discs were seen on some cars, capable of increasing braking efficiency. Now the drivers are capable of slowing down more than 220 kilometres per hour in the space of thirty metres. The new frontier for increasing braking power now appears to be berillium calipers, which have already been used in Grand Prixs and which are capable of improving heat dispersion, thereby speeding up the brake cooling.

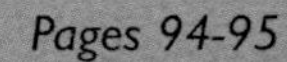

Pages 94-95
The last few minutes before the start of a Grand Prix. A band accompanies the "grid-girls", each one of which is holding the flag of the nationality of the driver who occupies a position on the grid. On the front row can be found the flag of the International Federation with alongside the banners of the national federation which organizes the Grand Prix in question and - whenever it does not clash - that of the host nation. Until one minute before the start, the grid is packed with mechanics, team managers, team and sponsor representatives, journalists and photographers. But when the final siren sounds, only the cars are left on the grid. When the five red lights are switched off, the cars start at a slow speed on their warm-up lap, the final one before the start of the race.

Pages 96-97
Side impact collision safety: this is one of the most recent innovations from the international federation, which has imposed cushioned sidewalls on both sides of the driver's helmets. The close-up photo is of 1996 world champion Damon Hill in his Arrows. In the small photo: the rear head-rest and part of the roll-bar behind the driver. According to the regulations, an imaginary line drawn between the highest point of the roll-bar and the front extremity of the cockpit opening must pass above the head of the driver.

GÜNTHER
SKL
GOODYEAR
GOODYEAR
TOTAL
sparco
s.Oliver

R.SCHUMACHER
Diavia

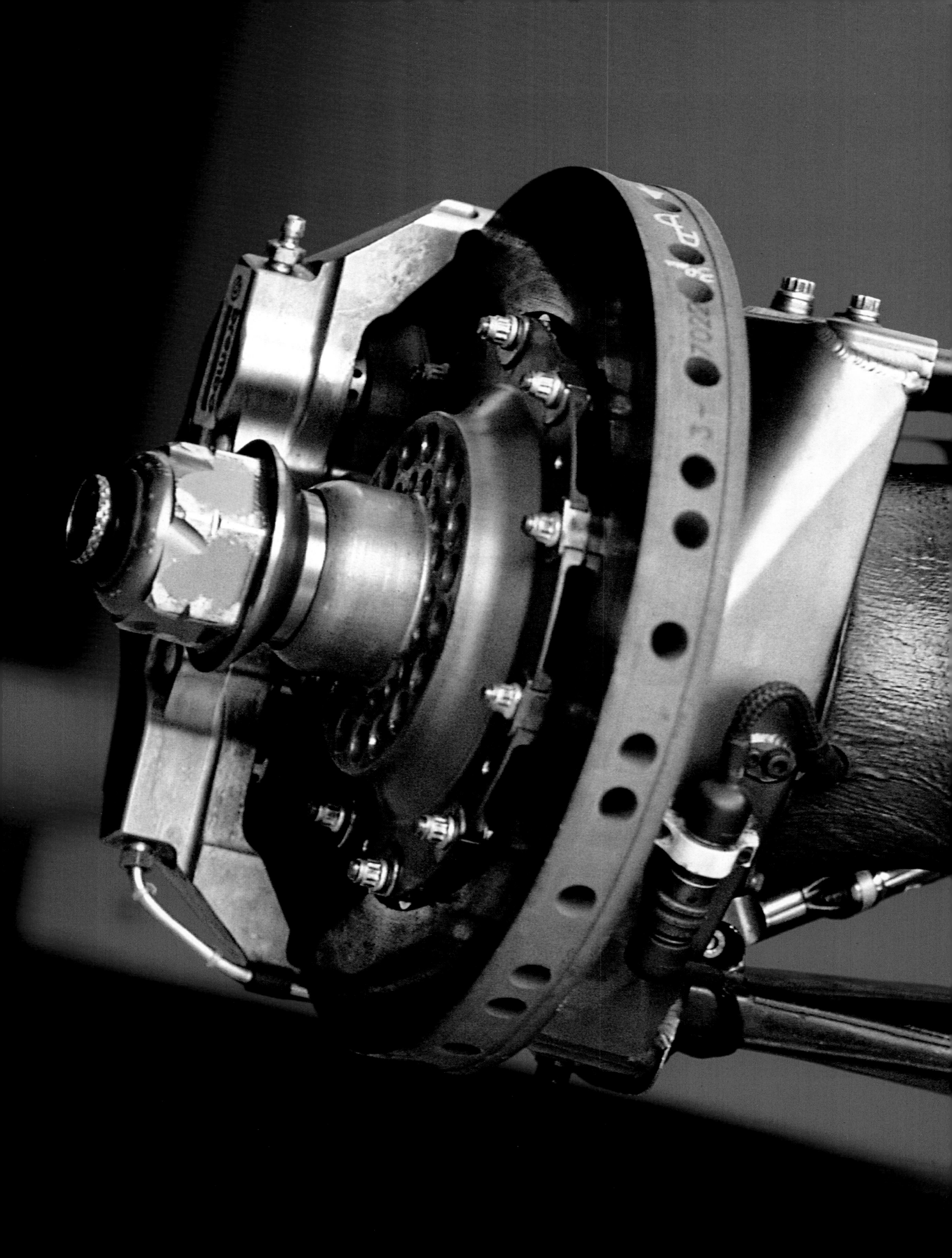

PROST GAULOISES
PETRONAS

SAFETY CAR
Mercedes-Benz
SAFETY CAR

Rothmans

Sabelt
Sabelt
Sabelt

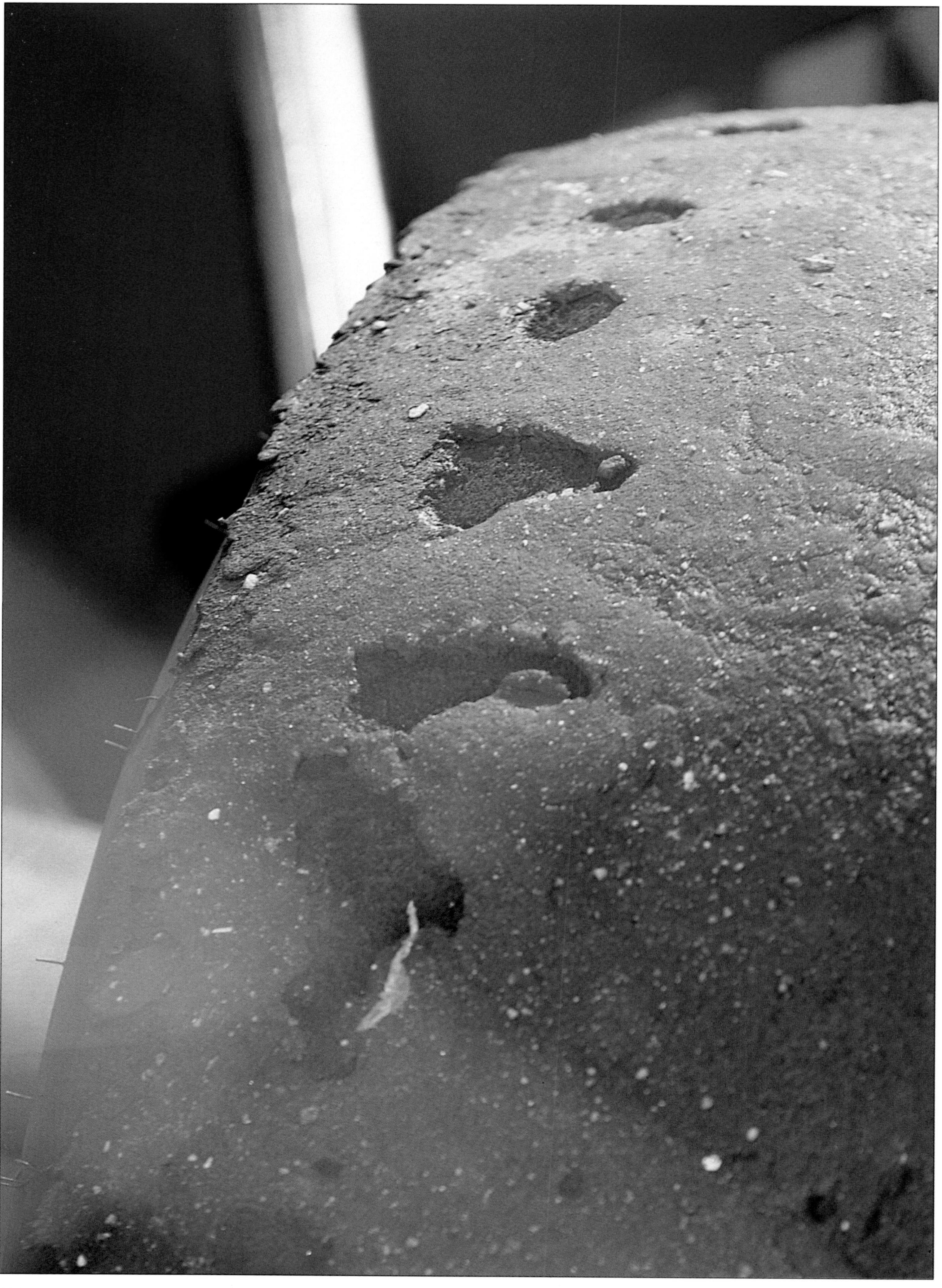

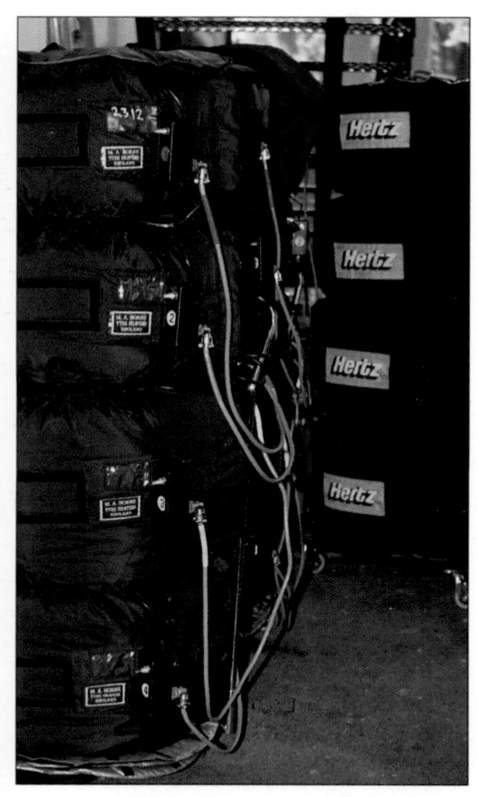

THE TYRES

It was clear at the start of the season that a renewed battle between the tyre manufacturers was going to revolutionize Formula 1, and not just performance-wise: the safety aspect was also important. The US manufacturer Goodyear had had a total monopoly in F1 since 1991. When Pirelli retired at the end of that season, the American giant began to supply tyres to everybody. This undoubtedly had positive effects from a safety point of view, because the tyres were identical for all and this was one less thing for the teams to

Tyres, tyres and more tyres. In the 1997 world championship, the "war" between Goodyear and the newly-arrived Bridgestone company led to a massive increase in tyre performance, but also to a drop in their duration. In several races, especially in the summer, the tyres showed signs of rapid and unpredictable (see side) deterioration, or even blistering (other page), that is anomalous and irregular formation of craters on the surface of the tread. For years now, a stable feature of pitlane activity has been the tyre-warmers to keep the tyres at the right remperature before they are fitted on to the car, which can in this way start the race with maximum efficiency and grip.

BRIDGESTONE
BBS
BRIDGESTONE

HEWLETT
PACKARD
EDS
Ford
The
MacNeal-Schwendler
Corporation
MSC
BRIDGESTONE
BBS

worry about. However this levelling factor led to a period of slumber in tyre development. Now Bridgestone's arrival in F1 has revolutionized the scene. The Japanese giant is serious about F1 and has invested heavily in research, design and testing. In 1996 it had already carried out numerous tests with large quantities of different tyres, and this led to a number of innovations above all in wet weather tyre development.

At this point the battle got underway. The US manufacturer, which had remained almost static in tyre development over the past couple of years, had to get involved in a massive testing and production programme. This led to the development of competitive new tyres but ones which were precarious on a reliability level. Let us look at the facts: for a number of years now, unusual tyre wear had almost been eliminated. In 1997, 'blistering'

My name's Bridgestone,
I come from Japan ...
One of the world's tyre manufacturing giants arrived in Formula in 1997, bringing a revolution to F1 after five seasons of total Goodyear monopoly, which began in 1991 after the withdrawl of Pirelli. The Bridgestone Grand Prix team is headed by project manager Yasukawa and tyres were supplied to Stewart, Prost and Arrows as well as to the team of Giancarlo Minardi (see side).

RSE
motion
RACING

(anomalous tread wear, with sometimes enormous bubbles and holes) and 'lamination' (when the carcass tread comes away from the tyre), were almost commonplace. Canada and Hungary were the two Grand Prixs in which Goodyear suffered the most. At Monza on the other hand, Bridgestone were in difficulty. But the constant factor which links Goodyear and Bridgestone tyres is above all performance. This has been exceptional throughout the year, sometimes with an improvement of four seconds per lap on the best times set on each circuit the year before. This is entirely due to the tyres and their new compounds and constructions, which are much more competitive than in the past. Often this has been to the advantage of competition on the track, with the 'tyre variable' now having an important part to play both in qualifying and the race. That's not all: this variable will play an even bigger part in the future, because the entry of French manufacturer Michelin is on the horizon ...

An engineer at work with paints on the brake discs of a Tyrrell. The different colours help to establish the amount of wear in a disc and also the maximum working temperature reached. The cost of a complete set of latest-generation brake discs for a Formula 1 car is over 10,000 dollars.

PIAA
EUROPEAN
AVIATION
EUROPEAN
AVIATION
GOODYEAR
GOODYEAR
EPSON
PARAMETRIC
ICL
18
PIAA
MORSE
MORSE
CHAMPION
Auto
Trader
REMOVE BEFORE FLIGHT

PIT-GARAGE SECRETS

Every year, Grand Prix life - at least from the point of view of driver-team relationships - has moved even further behind the often darkened windows of the ubiquitous motorhome. In these travelling offices, equipped with telephones, faxes and computers, the "tactical" aspects of F1 are thrashed out, while the rest of the team continue to work within the pit garage. Thirty years ago a pit garage was a sort of "box" (giving rise to the use of the word "box" meaning pit-garage in Italian) with four solid walls: a roof, two dividing walls and the ground. The other two, that is the parts which looked onto the road parallel to the track and behind onto the paddock, were open. Then, as time went by, these were closed by metal doors, cutting off paddock activity. It was impossible to separate the covered area from the pitlane, except for

The camera catches secrets of the pits. On the Ford Cosworth-powered Tyrrell of Jos Verstappen, engineers from the American engine manufacturer are in the most delicate phase of their work. With computers, they download all the engine data compiled by the numerous sensors within. With the same method, but in the other direction, computers manage to programme the various engine functions at different settings.

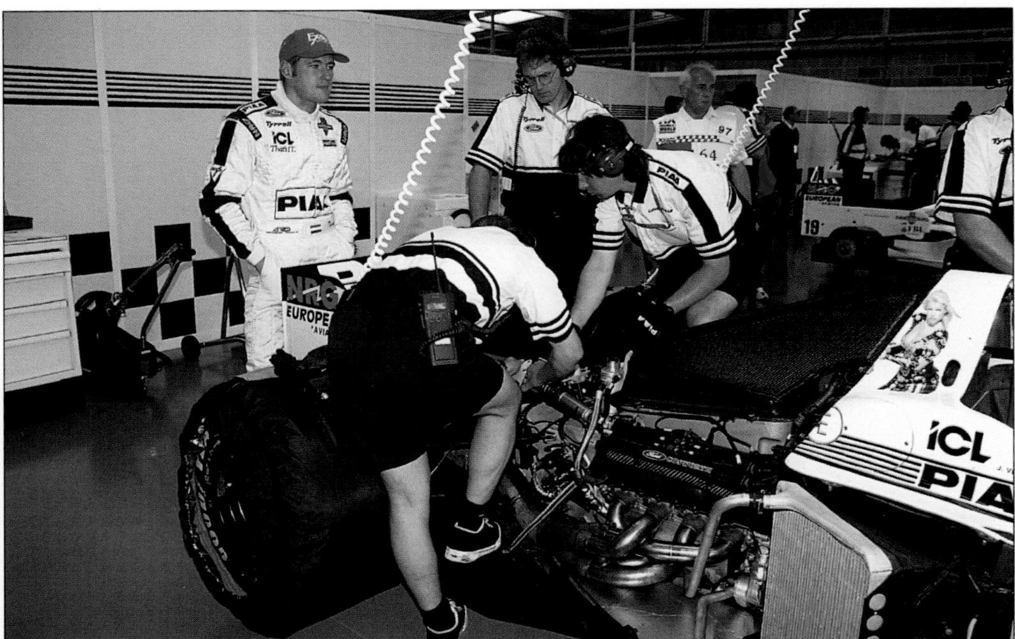

Tyrrell
PIAA
ICL
That's IT.
GOODYEAR
www.verstappen.nl

ICL
That's IT.

Tyrrell
PIAA
Auto Trader
MORSE

NRG
EUROPEAN
AVIATION
18
PIAA
ICL

Tyrrell
PIAA
EUROPEAN
ICL
Auto Trader
MORSE
MiTech

moments of maximum tension when the shutters were pulled down. At that point, tensa-barriers were invented to keep prying eyes away. Although these boxes were like large (not always, however) and unkempt garages, with different sizes and characteristics

Verstappen talks with an engineer while the mechanics are finishing the setting-up of his car. Final preparations: work on the rear suspension of the Tyrrell 025 and Jos follows closely. A few minutes wait, with his helmet already on, and then it's time to get into the car. Verstappen's mechanics tightens his belt while the engine cover is put in place. A final glance at the time-keeping monitor and then it's time to enter the track.

Exact
PIAA
Tyrrell
ICL
That's IT.
PIAA
EUROPEAN
AVIATION
Tyrrell

depending on the circuit, today things have been standardized. Current pit garages are always large and spacious, as clean as operating rooms, with various internal areas separated by mobile walls covered with sponsors' logos and names. In particular, this is to separate the secret rear part, where all sorts of activities not for the curious take place, from the working area which looks onto the pitlane. It is above all the area which houses the team computers and it is here that the screens display the exact data of all the modern technology that makes up today's F1 cars.

Although the rear can be called a sort of study area, it is in the front that the most important events occur before and after a driver goes out onto the track. In this space, usually about 5 by 12 metres in size are positioned, the three cars which make up the team. Race cars for the two drivers on the two sides; in the middle the spare car, usually set up for each driver in turn (except for those teams which have a number

Pit life at Tyrrell. Behind the rear wing, Verstappen follows the work on the rear end of his Tyrrell. On the left of the car can be seen the race car of Mika Salo, who is clearly on the track with his spare car, which is usually positioned in the middle of the garage. But for Verstappen, it is not yet time to take to the track: there is still some time for a walk and sign autographs.

I driver by contract, Michael Schumacher and Ferrari for example). There are very few occasions in which a team has four cars in the pit garage.
While briefings and technical meetings take place in the motorhomes, the cars are continually dismantled and put together again in order to change various components, to record data or to improve suspension set-up. Recently the time it takes to replace the main parts of the car has been reduced drastically: a couple of hours for a complete engine plus all its ancillary parts, just over an hour to change an engine. These operations are sometimes carried out under the watchful eye of the driver, who will maybe sit close to his mechanics in order to exchange vital information with his engineers.
There are also fine-tuning phases in which a technician with a laptop computer downloads data from the car or inserts it. If these operations happen during a practice or qualifying session, the driver follows them from outside the car until they have finished. At that point the driver, in his full gear, gets into the cockpit and is ready to exchange information about the car or the race via radio link, while he follows the images and data broadcast on a monitor placed in front of him. These are the final few seconds before qualifying or the race ... then, finally he can leave the pit garage. It's now all up to him!

Technical preparation is over. Verstappen, in his driving-suit and helmet, can now get into the cockpit of his Tyrrell, with a mechanic ready to place a monitor in front of him. The driver can follow the monitor while the mechanic makes the final adjustments to his safetybelt. Now everything is ready: with a roar from its Cosworth engine, the Tyrrell emerges from the pit garage and powers down the pitlane towards the track entrance.

Rothmans
FALKE
Rothmans
Rothmans
Rothmans
GOODYEAR

PIT-STOPS IN DETAIL

Maybe one day we will remember pit-stops as the lifeline for the F1 of the 1990s. On many occasions these complex tyre-changing and refuelling manoevres have offered the only opportunity for a change in the race standings. With modern-day pit-stops, major errors which have in the past conditioned the outcome of a race are not even necessary. For example, fuel hoses inserted badly into the cars, wheel-nuts fixed in a careless way or wheels which drop off even before the car has exited the pitlane. It remains a fact that tactics and strategies tied to these crucial moments have turned some teams into winners and others into losers. Ferrari, for example, has proved to be the fastest team in the pitlane on many occasions. Some races have in fact been decided by a pit-stop: Alesi lost this

A rapidly decelerating Williams is two metres away from the point where it will come to a halt for its pitstop. Sixteen highly-trained mechanics are waiting: one with the pit-board; two to raise and lower the car with the front and rear jacks; one refuelling mechanic; three for each wheel: one to work the compressed-air gun to unscrew and screw back on the wheel, one to take off the wheel with the used tyre and one to fit the new wheel.

Lockheed
Rothmans
FALKE

Rothmans
MIRAGE
Lockheed
FALKE
GOODYEAR

Rothmans

Rothmans

Rothmans
RENAULT
Castrol
Rothmans
FALKE
MIRAGE
Rothmans

year's Italian GP because of a slower pitstop than Coulthard (McLaren) who was following him and who would probably never have overtaken him had it not been for the two cars' pitstops. There is nothing strange therefore if pit-stop tactics have become a race within a race. A total of 16 people are involved in the operation: the crew chief signals to the driver exactly where to stop the car; two mechanics deal with the jacking up of the car (one in front and one behind); one inserts the refuelling hose into the car, thus activating the pump mechanism; three mechanics replace each one of the tyres - one with an air-gun to unscrew and screw on the

Pages 114-115
A Williams pit-stop: four key moments from left to right, above and below. Frentzen has just stopped and the refuelling nozzle is immediately inserted in the filler on the right of the cockpit. Above right, it can be noted that the right-front tyre is the first one to be replaced. While the other three are being replaced, refuelling is still being carried out...

Once refuelling has been completed, the pit-board mechanic gets out of the way of the Williams. Frentzen can accelerate away, but he must not exceed the pitlane speed limit. The total time for a pit-stop varies from between 6 and a half seconds to 10 seconds, depending on the amount of fuel put in the car.

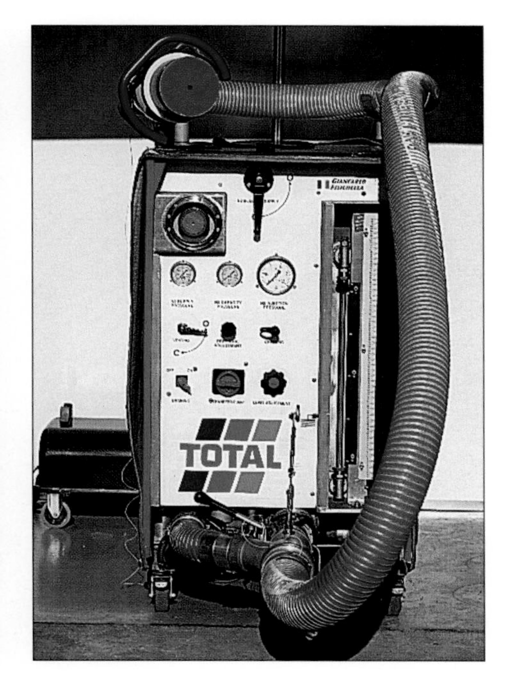

wheel-nut, one who removes the used tyre and one mechanic who puts on a new one.
Coordination in the operation of this task force has been gone over and over again dozens of times during private testing and often during pre-race practice sessions. In each GP in fact, a pit-stop can be repeated two or three times; irrespective of any errors, if a handful of seconds are saved on each occasion, the time taken can be very crucial for the outcome of a race. Another aspect is the risks of having to work with high-pressure refuelling apparatus. A fuel leak in the pits can have devastating effects, but even a slight loss of fuel from the nozzle can cause a fire to start when the driver goes back onto the track. With these problems, races are not the only things which can be lost: the stakes are even higher ...

A pit-stop for the Stewart Sf1 of Rubens Barrichello. The refuelling mechanic, Paul Singlehurst, is wearing a fire-protective helmet and overalls. Above: details of the Jordan refuelling equipment. The system, which respects F1 technical regulations and which is the same for all teams, refuels at a rate of about 10 litres a second.

Marlboro
BOSS
Mercedes
West
West
COMPUTER ASSOCIATES
West

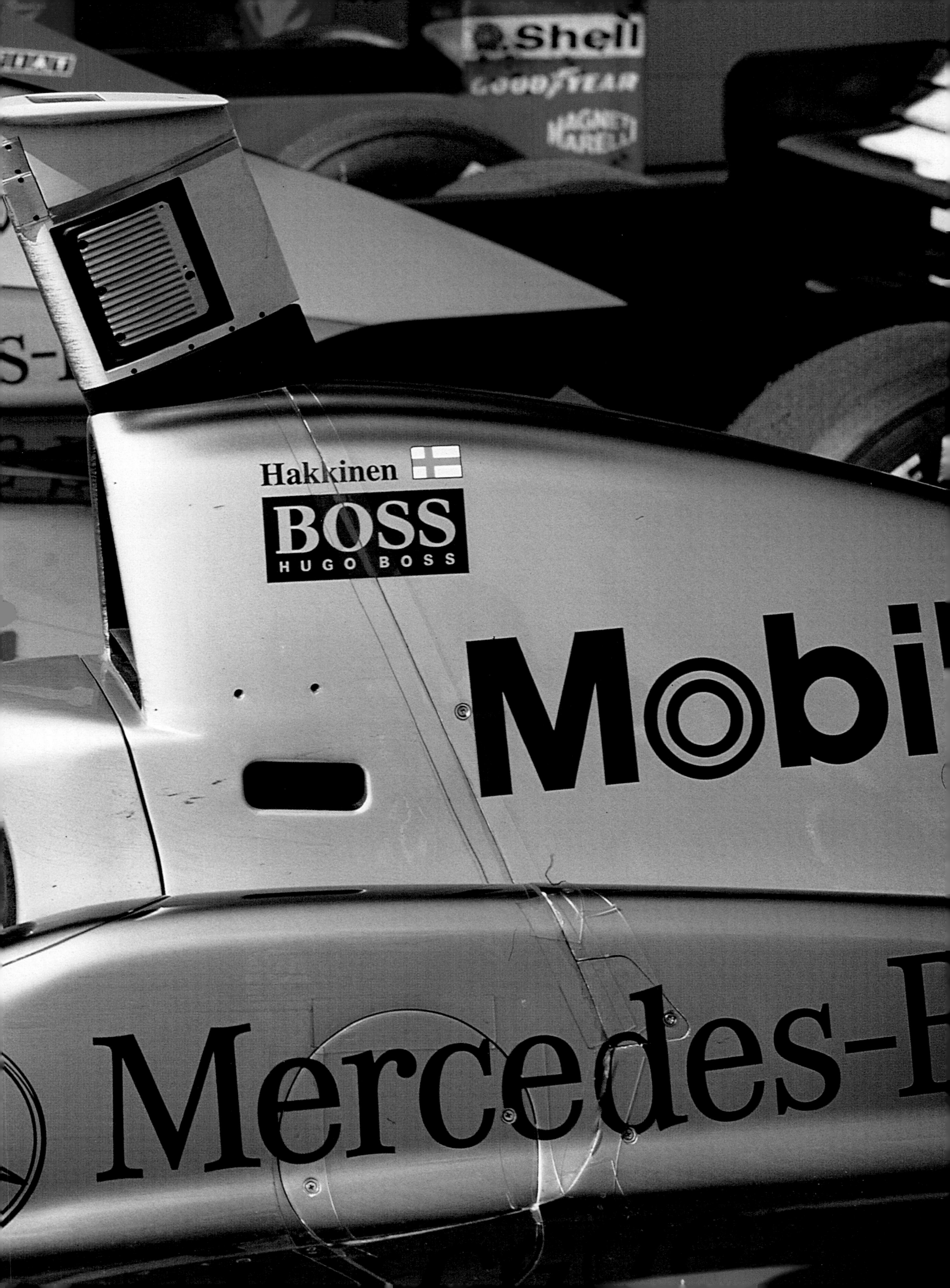

Shell
GOODYEAR
Hakkinen
BOSS
HUGO BOSS

Tyrrell
Ford
Ken Tyrrell
Marlboro
SF

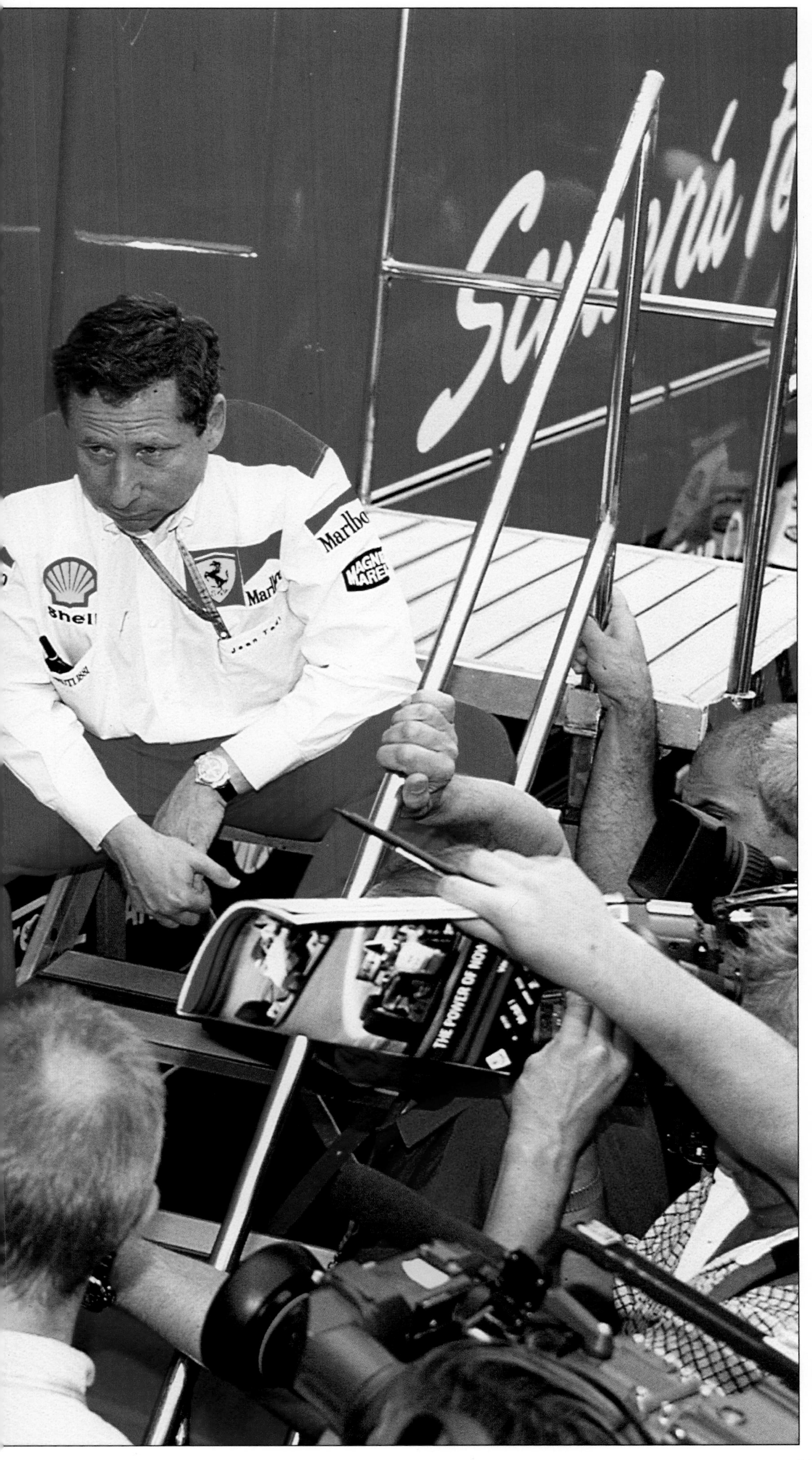

WOMEN AND VIPS

OK, it has to be admitted. There is no hiding the fact that the paddock, which is to be understood as the place around which Grand Prix life revolves, is unfortunately very different from what the man in the street imagines it to be. Behind the pit garages (which are always off-limits for anyone who is not a driver, engineer or mechanic), the large area taken up by the massive motorhomes or articulated lorries containing the race equipment, has increasingly become the haunt of 'wheeler-dealers', agents and marketing men rather than the general public. Even a glimpse of the drivers can only be caught now and again. From the pits to the motorhomes, from the motorhomes to the team briefings; from here back to the pits, with meals no longer consumed in the hospitality areas, as was the case a few years ago, but inside the motorhomes which are off-limits for the press, fans or the simply curious.

The two faces of the 1997 Ferrari: a group of journalists around Michael Schumacher looking for an interview, while team manager Jean Todt follows with interest. And Bernie Ecclestone, the "boss" of Formula 1, follows the red cars with particular attention...

marca oficial do GP

In a certain sense, the desire of the drivers for total privacy (the 'top' ones; the others sometimes can be seen mingling amongst the fans) has liberated the paddock area solely for business. The hospitality tents of the teams have become 'no-go' areas for those working in F1 and more for business acquaintances. Guests are invited to the luxurious surroundings of the Paddock Club, an area which has increased in size year by year, where teams and sponsors - those who can afford it - organize five-star lunches and get their drivers to participate in question/answer sessions. It is here that the most important representatives of this 'clan' are met by team managers who can lay the groundwork for new and lucrative contracts by exploiting the excitement of the moment.
This is the reason why the beautiful women and so-called VIPs are gradually disappearing from the paddock, which has become more of a business arena and less a place for teams and drivers.

Nelson Piquet, F1 world champion in 1981, '83 and '87, smiling at... the abundance of this splendid model, a guest of the Jordan team. Less of a smile for Flavio Briatore, talking in two different moments with his drivers Gerhard Berger and Jean Alesi. The Benetton team manager left at the end of 1997, after nine seasons with the team.

Not so long ago, Formula 1 was teeming with beautiful women, either driver girlfriends or representing sponsors or companies. Today this is no longer the case. The arrival of Sylvester Stallone at Monza or ex-princess Sarah Ferguson at Silverstone were the 'society highlights' of the 1997 Grand Prix season. Even in this case, visits do not take place on the casual basis of previous years; now they are organized down to the last detail, with muscular bodyguards for protection and a traditional visit to the secretive grey motorhome which dominates the paddock: this is the command centre of Bernie Ecclestone, the real owner of the modern-day Formula 1 which has become his private terrain. This 'closed-shop' community can only be reached by those who possess the famous magnetic pass which opens the automatic gates at the entrance to the paddock. The way things are going, in the future these gates are threatening to open less and less and passes are destined to become increasingly rare ...

In the Formula 1 pits these days, there is less colour and less of a happy atmosphere. That's why Eddie Jordan looks happy at the side of this beautiful model dressed in the colours of his team. When the girls poses alongside the Jordan 197, for a few moments the Silverstone pitlane becomes paralysed.

TOTAL
HEWLETT PACKARD
SSES
UGEOT
MENNA
TARTARIN
Startek
HISSES
12
GOODYEAR
EAGLE

FORMULA SAFETY

There are dozens of articles which control active and passive safety in the F1 regulations: those regarding the mechanical safety of the car are strictly regulated by a series of weights and measures, simulated crash-test procedures which reproduce with total precision an impact on every risk zone of a car in order to verify passive resistance. The same can be said for the driver's outfit, which must comply above all with international fire-resistant norms for each part of the body, helmet, gloves and boots included. Each different aspect of a Grand Prix weekend is today subject to precise norms and regulations, valid for all circuits, for all races and for every different condition.
Above all, the safety marshalls out on the circuit. As the years go by, the numbers increase and they become increasingly specialized, increasingly visible and identifiable thanks to coloured suits and tabards which are identical for

A panoramic view of the Monza pits seen from above on Italian GP weekend. In 1997 the so-called VIPs could not miss out on Formula 1 at the British GP, all attention was reserved for Sarah Ferguson; in Germany it was the turn of tennis champion Boris Becker, who showed great interest and knowledge in the Grand Prix world.

every race on the championship calendar, whether in Brazil, Italy or Japan. These marshalls have three main tasks: observe with the maximum of attention every phase of the race from their location, so that they can report incidents or disputes to Race Control; indicate to drivers by means of different-coloured flags what they must do in various situations (oil on the track, cars stopped in dangerous positions, qualifying/race interrupted): intervene as quickly as possible in case of incident or trip into the gravel and remove the driver from the cockpit or collaborate with the removal of the car. Nothing on the track is left to chance or free interpretation. The colour of the flags or their posi-

Different elements of circuit safety. A close-up of the sand-traps which slow the cars down in the run-off areas on the outside of which can often be found the old system of used tyres, which ensure the final protection. The kerbs are different on each circuit: in some rare cases, they also include extra vertical obstacles to prevent drivers from cutting corners or chicanes; they often have an irregular surface, making the car vibrate and forcing the driver to slow down if he passes over them. Above: sometimes the guard-rails are of the old type, but in circuits such as Montecarlo, special water-filled barriers which can absorb massive impacts are successfully used.

Ford
Tyrrell
ICL
That's IT.

GOODYEAR

ww.verstappen.nl

C.E.A.

tions (fixed, waved, held firm) means exactly one thing and nothing else, according to a written code which during every pre-race briefing is explained to the drivers by the race director.
The next chapter is the circuits. Even in this case, every minor detail has been thrashed out. The kerbs, for example, are coloured white and red at every F1 circuit so that they can be seen. Their height varies, but not excessively so that the car undertrays are not damaged when they go off the track. In any case, all the kerbs are now almost always ribbed, a further deterrent because of the vibrations for the drivers to use them as an extension of the track

Pages 132-133
Jos Verstappen's driving-suit, helmet and gloves. As well as ensuring maximum comfort for the driver, each item of racewear, helmet included, must comply with specific fire-resistant norms.

But is not only items of racewear which are used to combat fire. On many circuits, an important role in this sense is played by marshalls from the CEA: an Italian fire extinguisher firm which is famous throughout the world. Those with good memories may recall the miraculous intervention by CEA fire-marshalls at the 1989 San Marino GP, when Gerhard Berger was pulled out of his blazing Ferrari 640 in just a few seconds after he crashed into the wall at the Tamburello curve.

surface. There are few cases in which the kerbs have fixed obstacles, in order to deter drivers from cutting corners (as in the case of the infamous piles of tyres at Monza 1996, which were removed the year after).
The final chapter regards official track cars. The car of Sid Watkins, FIA Chief Doctor for the world championship, is highly visible and almost always red. It only enters the track if qualifying or the race is interrupted, or during the race, but in this case as a safety-car, equipped with flashing lights should there be an incident or stopped in a dangerous position.

Ralf Schumacher emerges unhurt from his Jordan after going off in the Canadian circuit of Montreal. Barrichello crashes and destroys the front right suspension of his Stewart. Thanks to the strength of the car and the large run-off areas present in almost every circuit toghether with the deceleration characteristics of these areas, today it is rare to see drivers involved in dangerous incidents.

Pages 138-139
Flag, tabards, colours, symbols. Today in F1, everything is precisely regulated for safety reasons. The yellow flags are vitally important: when waved, they mean that the driver cannot overtake on that occasion. The consequences (see Michael Schumacher in Australia) for drivers can be 10 seconds stop-and-go penalty in the pits or even disqualification.

02527
97 INTERLAGOS
FOTOSPEED

BOSS
Mobil 1
Mercedes-Benz
West
GOODYEAR

97
14016

CAMPARI
'6064
1997 MONZA
16055
1997 MONZA

AUTODROMO NAZIONALE MONZA
DOCTOR
5

VOLVO
Mobil 1
West

A Benetton powers past the sea at Montecarlo at 200Kph. In the Principality, even with the particular conditions of the street circuit, safety measures are particular and extremely efficient.

150

Rothmans
Rothmans

The safety-car has the job of neutralizing the race by slowing the drivers down and making them line up behind in single file until the flashing lights on the roof are switched off. At this point the safety car enters the pits and the race continues as normal.

Drivers racing, drivers relaxing. Michael Schumacher runs to the pits holding his helmet. Rubens Barrichello mediates, his helmet in his hand, after a problem with his Stewart-Ford. But the tranquillizing effect of the Oscar Galvez circuit in Argentina is fantastic for Heinz-Harald Frentzen, who decides to have a snooze under a tree after being let down by his car!

Pages 144-145
Seventeen races, thousands of curves, millions of dollars of sponsorship... They couldn't exist without the passion which has always surrounded F1. The shining example of this "fever" is the "Hill of Passion" before the Variante Bassa at Imola. A hill which for three days becomes the scene for enthusiasm, shouting, joy and even anger. On Sunday evening the place looks deserted and sad. See you all again in one year's time...

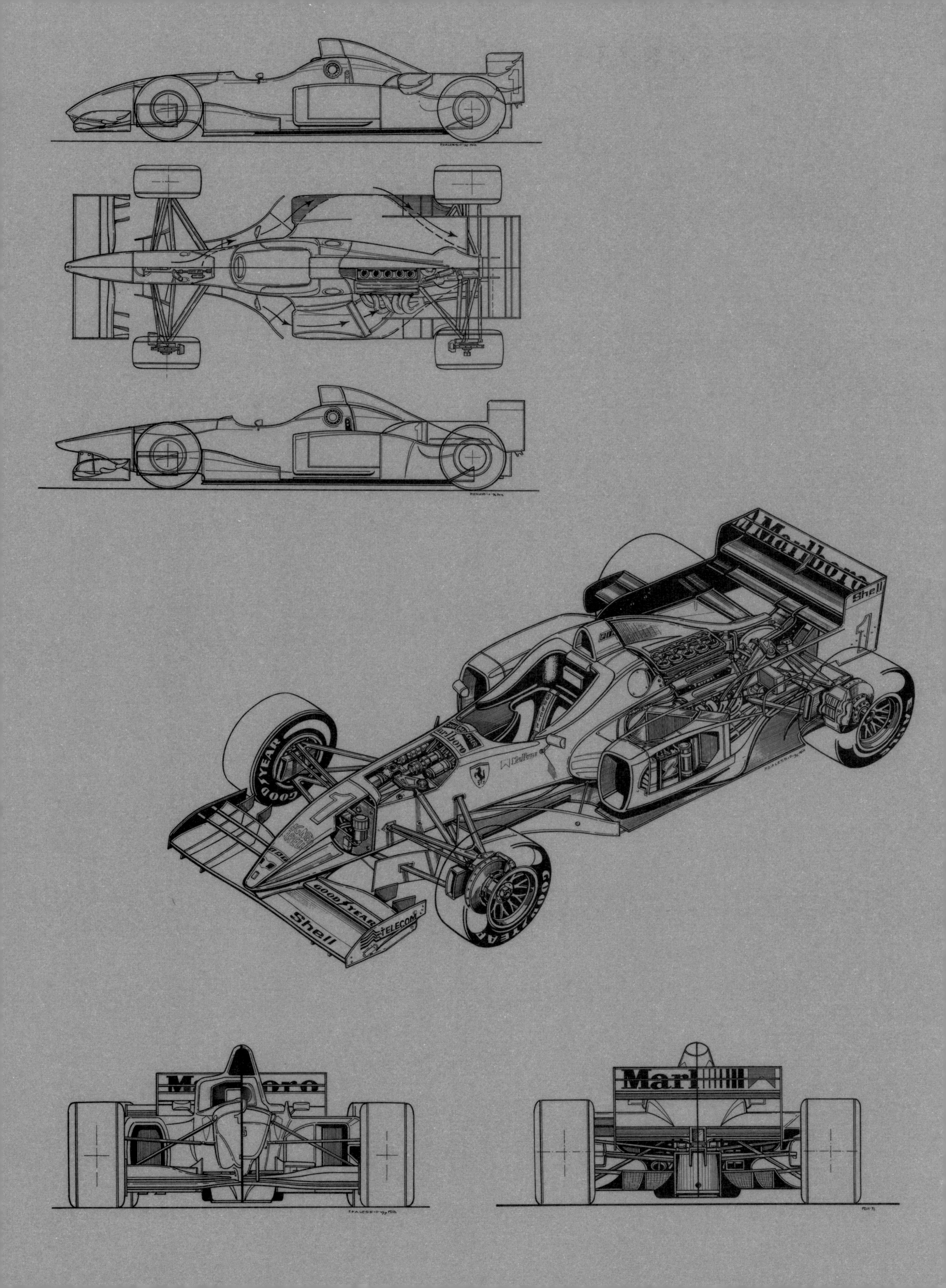

Marlboro
Shell
1
GOOD YEAR
Shell
TELECOM

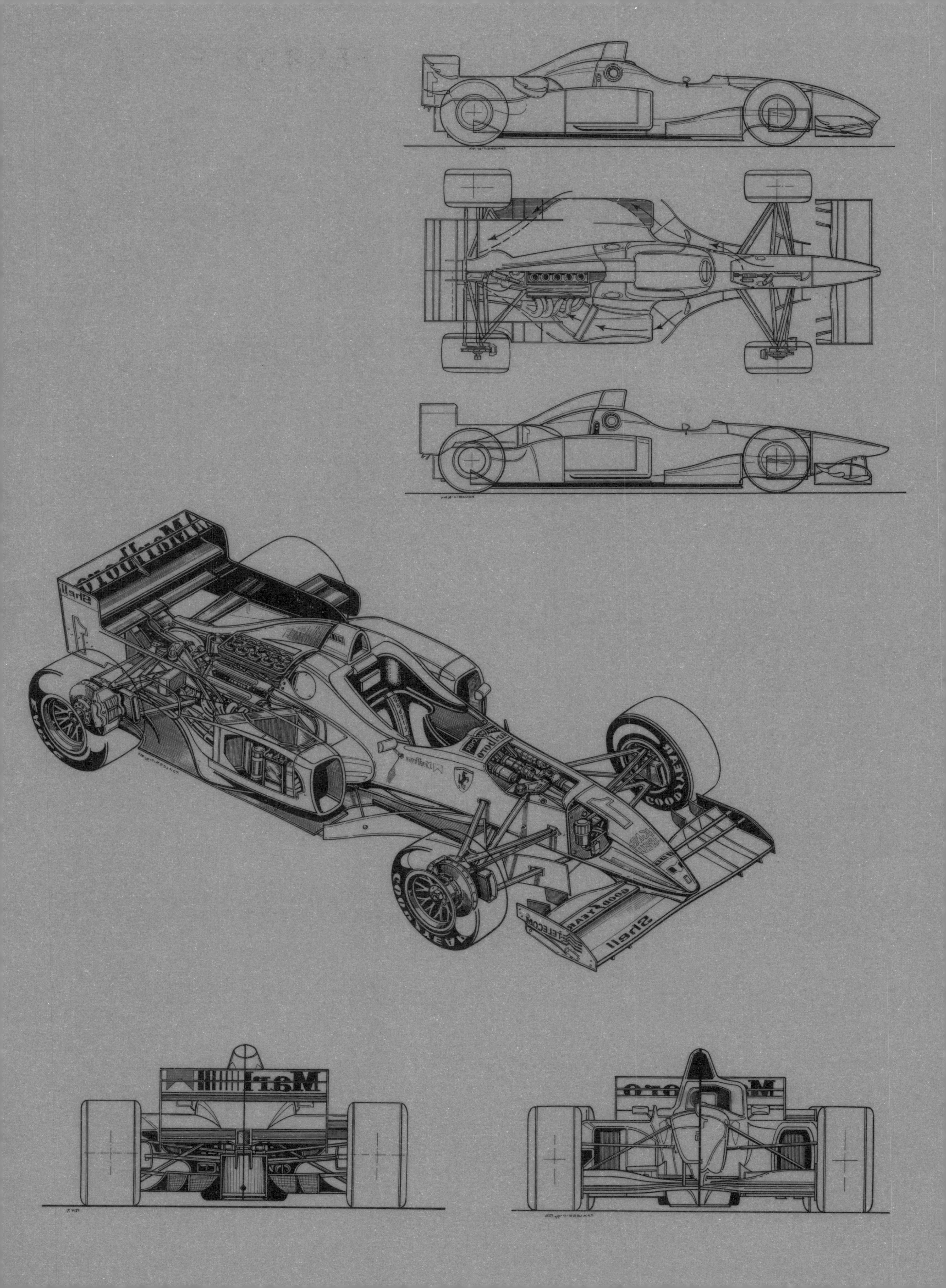

TELECOM
Shell

FERRARI F310B

1997 was supposed to be the turning-point for Ferrari. In a season when it celebrated its 50th anniversary, the Prancing Horse finally returned to the top, on the same level as Benetton, Williams and McLaren, the cars which had relegated the Italian cars to a secondary role in recent years.

After a long period of mediocrity, sporadic exploits and a total lack of reliability and results, a competitive Ferrari was finally seen; a Ferrari which was capable of aiming regularly for the podium, or even for victory. A large part of the merit for this resurrection can be attributed to Michael Schumacher, the best driver around at the moment and the only driver who can really make a difference. It can also be attributed to the management at Maranello, which in the past few years has created a fresh structure for the

1) In order to give a better impression of the results obtained by Ferrari throughout 1997, we must take one step backwards and compare the current car with last year's model. This time light years separate the two projects from each other, not the traditional 12 months. The first Ferrari powered by a 10 cylinder engine was characterized by unusual aerodynamics. The nose, unlike all the other F1 cars, was raised and anchored with a sole central column. The sides had elliptical-shaped air intakes and were separate from the central part of the car, as on the unsuccessful F92A from 1992. These numerous aerodynamic innovations, concentrated in a new model, ended up by having a negative effect on the performance of the F310, which only won the Spanish GP in this configuration. Starting from Canada, the red cars were heavily modified and the 'ant-eater' nose was replaced by a more conventional one, similar to those used by the competition.

2) In summer 1996, John Barnard was given an ultimatum: enough of genial inventions and original cars at all costs. For 1997 Ferrari needed a simple, reliable car which was easy to set up. The designer did not agree but had to obey. The result of lengthy wind-tunnel aerodynamic work was the F310B, a simple, apparently ordinary-looking car. Many people defined it immediately as a 'red Williams'. There were in fact many similarities between the new car from Maranello and the 1996 championship-winning Williams. The '97 Ferrari lost its sinuous shape and the lateral elliptical-shaped air intakes and became more squared-off. This aerodynamic configuration was half-way between a Williams (nose, front sides and engine air intake shape) and a Benetton (design of the sides).

FERRARI F310B

1997 was supposed to be the turning-point for Ferrari. In a season when it celebrated its 50th anniversary, the Prancing Horse finally returned to the top, on the same level as Benetton, Williams and McLaren, the cars which had relegated the Italian cars to a secondary role in recent years.

After a long period of mediocrity, sporadic exploits and a total lack of reliability and results, a competitive Ferrari was finally seen; a Ferrari which was capable of aiming regularly for the podium, or even for victory. A large part of the merit for this resurrection can be attributed to Michael Schumacher, the best driver around at the moment and the only driver who can really make a difference. It can also be attributed to the management at Maranello, which in the past few years has created a fresh structure for the

1) In order to give a better impression of the results obtained by Ferrari throughout 1997, we must take one step backwards and compare the current car with last year's model. This time light years separate the two projects from each other, not the traditional 12 months. The first Ferrari powered by a 10 cylinder engine was characterized by unusual aerodynamics. The nose, unlike all the other F1 cars, was raised and anchored with a sole central column. The sides had elliptical-shaped air intakes and were separate from the central part of the car, as on the unsuccessful F92A from 1992. These numerous aerodynamic innovations, concentrated in a new model, ended up by having a negative effect on the performance of the F310, which only won the Spanish GP in this configuration. Starting from Canada, the red cars were heavily modified and the 'ant-eater' nose was replaced by a more conventional one, similar to those used by the competition.

2) In summer 1996, John Barnard was given an ultimatum: enough of genial inventions and original cars at all costs. For 1997 Ferrari needed a simple, reliable car which was easy to set up. The designer did not agree but had to obey. The result of lengthy wind-tunnel aerodynamic work was the F310B, a simple, apparently ordinary-looking car. Many people defined it immediately as a 'red Williams'. There were in fact many similarities between the new car from Maranello and the 1996 championship-winning Williams. The '97 Ferrari lost its sinuous shape and the lateral elliptical-shaped air intakes and became more squared-off. This aerodynamic configuration was half-way between a Williams (nose, front sides and engine air intake shape) and a Benetton (design of the sides).

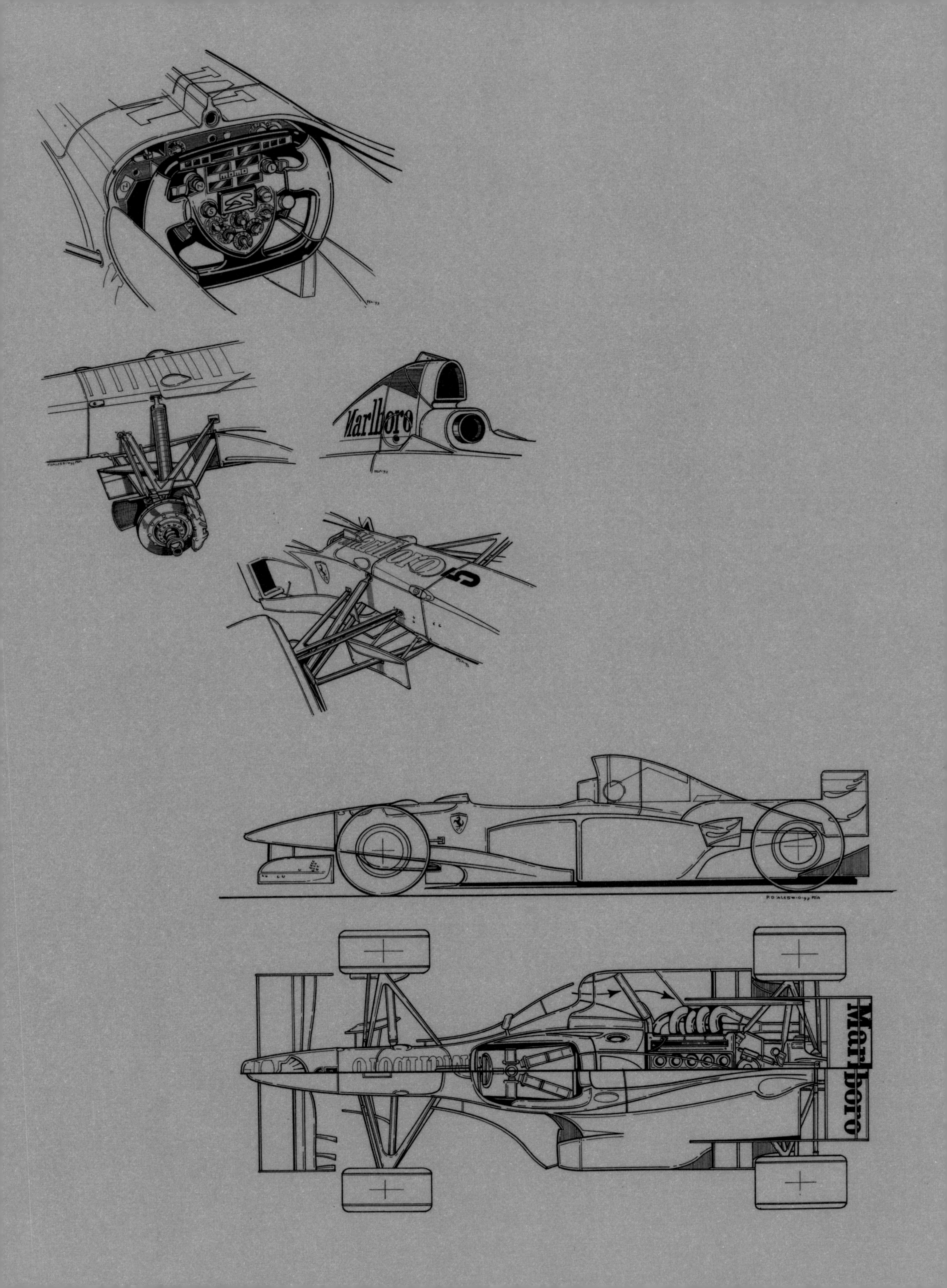

Marlboro

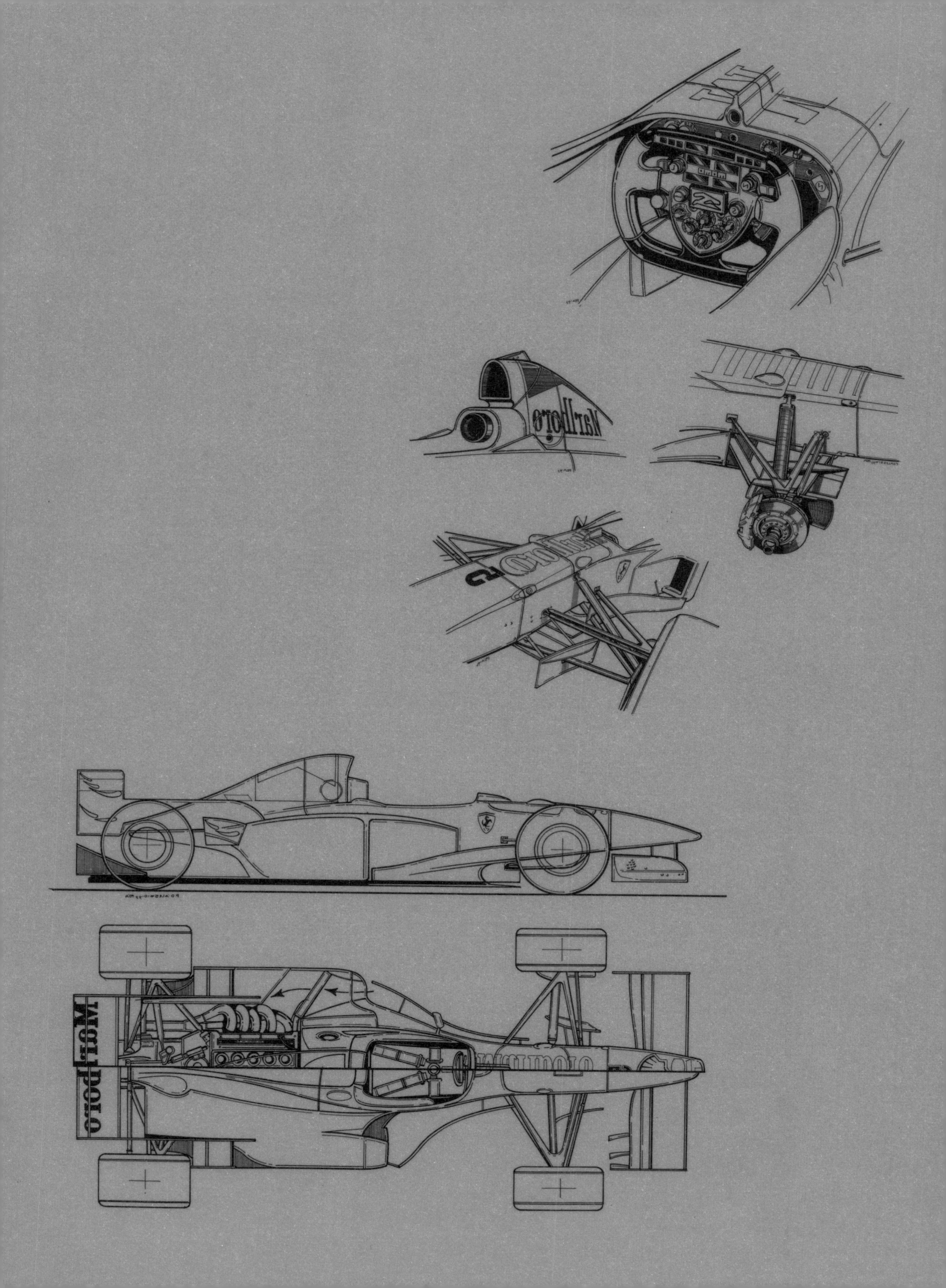

most famous team in the world. After the end of John Barnard and the technological centre over the English Channel, the Ferrari of the end-of-the-century has returned to the old style by concentrating all racing team structures at Maranello. The unpredictable British designer has been replaced by Rory Byrne and Ross Brawn, two outstanding engineers who have made a decisive contribution to the rebirth of the Prancing Horse.

3) The F310B had a number of original ideas such as a complex steering-wheel, which is to all intents and purposes a mobile flight-deck. The main commands can be easily reached by the driver, who can change a total of 10 different settings.

In order to find out the real face of Ferrari, we will have to wait for the 1998 season, when finally a car will be produced by this new engineering line-up. This should be the car which Ferrari fans all over the world have been expecting for a long time. The 1997 F310B, despite being a worthy single-seater, has never been perfect. It could be defined as an honest F1 workhorse, which compensated for some of the many errors made during the 1996 season. Very reliable and quite versatile, the F310B has perfectly adapted to the characteristics of some circuits with a slippery track surface, but has been in difficulty on ultra-fast tracks, where it has never been able to keep up with the best. This was because its poor aerodynamic design cancelled out the advantages gained in engine performance, making all the efforts of Schumacher and Irvine in vain. On some occasions, the performances of the red cars were worse than

4) The Ferrari F310B was the car which underwent the most modifications during 1997. When Rory Byrne and Ross Brawn arrived at Maranello at the start of the year, they wanted to revise the Barnard project, but there wasn't enough time. They therefore modified everything that could be modified: the shape of the front wing, the design of the sides (starting from the French GP the small wings ahead of the driving wheels on the Ferrari disappeared). Then the shape of the rear exhaust profile, the engine air intake as well as the design of the front suspension, which from the German GP onwards incorporated a number of faired elements which also had an aerodynamic function.

most famous team in the world. After the end of John Barnard and the technological centre over the English Channel, the Ferrari of the end-of-the-century has returned to the old style by concentrating all racing team structures at Maranello. The unpredictable British designer has been replaced by Rory Byrne and Ross Brawn, two outstanding engineers who have made a decisive contribution to the rebirth of the Prancing Horse.

In order to find out the real face of Ferrari, we will have to wait for the 1998 season, when finally a car will be produced by this new engineering line-up. This should be the car which Ferrari fans all over the world have been expecting for a long time. The 1997 F310B, despite being a worthy single-seater, has never been perfect. It could be defined as an honest F1 workhorse, which compensated for some of the many errors made during the 1996 season. Very reliable and quite versatile, the F310B has perfectly adapted to the characteristics of some circuits with a slippery track surface, but has been in difficulty on ultra-fast tracks, where it has never been able to keep up with the best. This was because its poor aerodynamic design cancelled out the advantages gained in engine performance, making all the efforts of Schumacher and Irvine in vain. On some occasions, the performances of the red cars were worse than

3) The F310B had a number of original ideas such as a complex steering-wheel, which is to all intents and purposes a mobile flight-deck. The main commands can be easily reached by the driver, who can change a total of 10 different settings.

4) The Ferrari F310B was the car which underwent the most modifications during 1997. When Rory Byrne and Ross Brawn arrived at Maranello at the start of the year, they wanted to revise the Barnard project, but there wasn't enough time. They therefore modified everything that could be modified: the shape of the front wing, the design of the sides (starting from the French GP the small wings ahead of the driving wheels on the Ferrari disappeared). Then the shape of the rear exhaust profile, the engine air intake as well as the design of the front suspension, which from the German GP onwards incorporated a number of faired elements which also had an aerodynamic function.

arlboro
Marlboro
EAGLE
GOODYEAR
GOODYEA
GOODYEA
Shell
Shell
5
rlboro

the two Saubers, which had 1996 Ferrari engines. Another congenital defect of the F310B was turn-in problems which on some tracks (especially those with an average speed of more than 200 kph) translated into excessive tyre wear and early deterioration. This wear cost Schumacher victory at the Hungarian GP and relegated the Ferraris to a supporting role in the much-awaited Italian GP.
One of the partially negative points on Ferrari's 1997 balance-sheet is the engine. The Italian team, which finished the 1996 championship at the top, in just 12 months managed to lose all the advantage it had over the competition. After the first races in the calendar, the 10 cylinder 046 'step 1' was to have been replaced by a revised, more powerful version, called 'step 2'. This new engine only appeared at the French GP (the last one of the first half of the season), but without the increase in performance the drivers expected which was necessary for the final battle against Ferrari's rivals in the crucial phase of the championship.

the two Saubers, which had 1996 Ferrari engines. Another congenital defect of the F310B was turn-in problems which on some tracks (especially those with an average speed of more than 200 kph) translated into excessive tyre wear and early deterioration. This wear cost Schumacher victory at the Hungarian GP and relegated the Ferraris to a supporting role in the much-awaited Italian GP.
One of the partially negative points on Ferrari's 1997 balance-sheet is the engine. The Italian team, which finished the 1996 championship at the top, in just 12 months managed to lose all the advantage it had over the competition. After the first races in the calendar, the 10 cylinder 046 'step 1' was to have been replaced by a revised, more powerful version, called 'step 2'. This new engine only appeared at the French GP (the last one of the first half of the season), but without the increase in performance the drivers expected which was necessary for the final battle against Ferrari's rivals in the crucial phase of the championship.

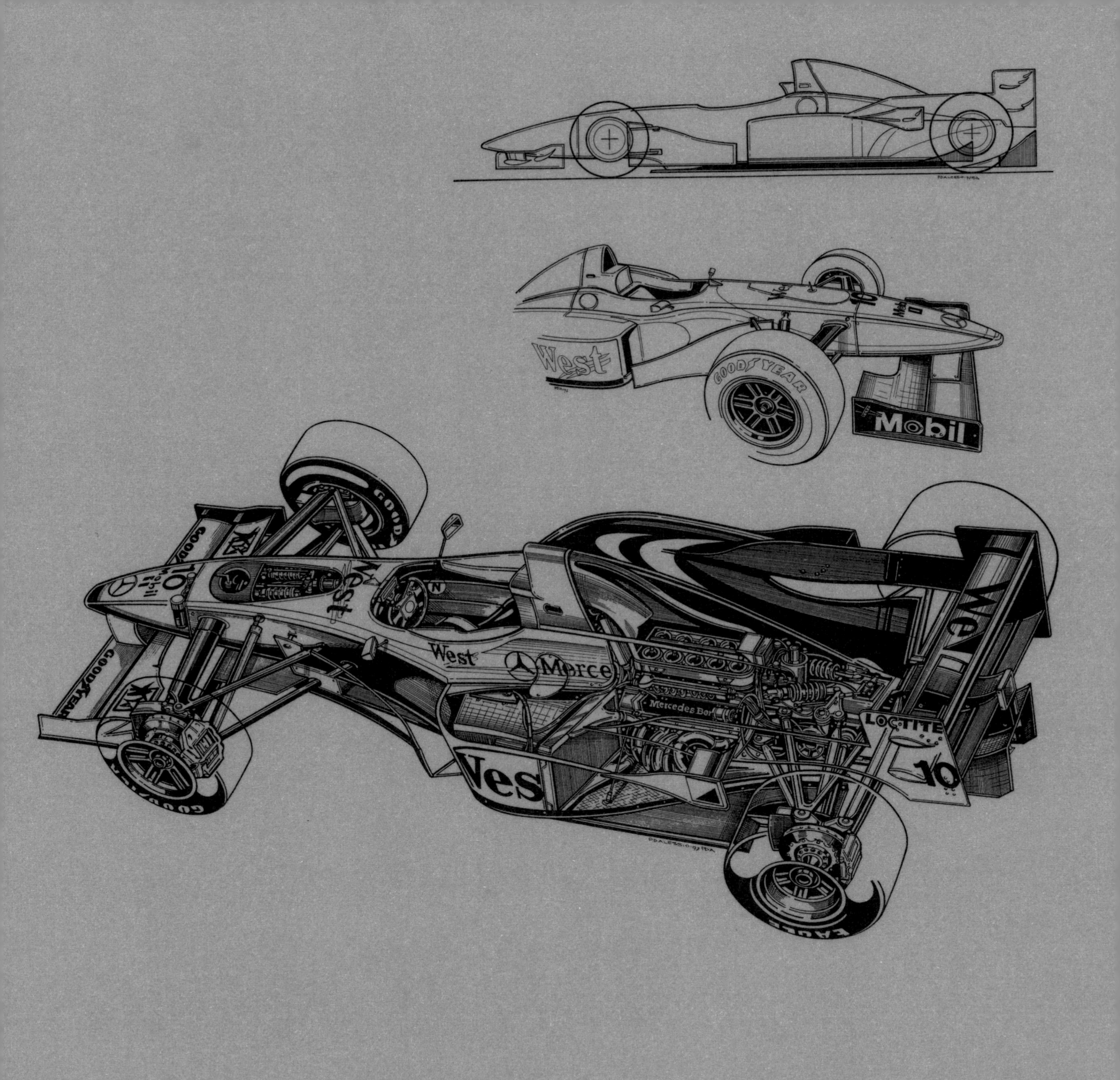
West
GOODYEAR
Mobil
West
Merce
LOCTITE
10

McLAREN MERCEDES MP4/12

1997 was also a year of resurrection for team McLaren-Mercedes. After three seasons without a win, poor performances and numerous retirements, Ron Dennis' team finally returned to victory and its traditional F1 role. When, after just one season with the 10 cylinder Peugeot engine, McLaren and Mercedes announced their 'marriage', for the Anglo-German team it was thought that they would be back on the top by 1995. But in modern-day F1, it is not enough just to be called McLaren or Mercedes to guarentee oneself a place in the sun. The ultra-modern technology of today's F1 requires longer periods, careful planning and top-level management. These in turn require two or three seasons before the results start to show. That is why the return of Ron Dennis' team to the victory rostrum, three years after its last Grand Prix win by Ayrton Senna in Australia 1993, increasingly bears the name of Mercedes. Together with the Peugeot engine, the German V10 unit (developed by Mario Illien) is considered to be the most powerful in today's F1 line-up. In its qualifying version, rumours abound of 800 bhp, while the race version should be around 750 bhp. These engine figures, together with good reliability, have enabled McLaren to return amongst the top teams. Although the balance-sheet on the engineering side is in the black, the same cannot be said for the McLaren. The MP4/12 had an acceptable chassis, but its aerodynamics left a lot to be desired.On fast tracks for example, Coulthard and Hakkinen raced with enormous rear wings, a sign of little rear downforce. Furthermore the McLaren was the only '97 car to retain high cockpit sides (introduced last year to protect the head of the driver in case of side impact), which certainly do not help performance. Not to mention the complex bulkheads on the sides of the front wheels, which were greeted with a thumbs-down by many rival designers. The situation in any case will probably improve in 1998 with the arrival within the team of the genial Adrian Newey, the designer whom Ron Dennis lured away from Williams. Newey is probably the best engineer currently in F1. He was responsible for some of the most significant cars of the past few years. When he was still a 'rookie' designer at March-Leyton House, he introduced the idea of a tapered chassis at the front and a raised nose. When he arrived at Williams, he contributed to the development of the unbeatable FW12B, the active-suspension car which dominated the 1992 season with Ni-

1) The same could be said about McLaren as Benetton. In 1997 the team designers limited themselves to just refining the previous year's project, concentrating attention above all on engine development. That is why the aerodynamics remained virtually unchanged and why McLaren was the only top team to maintain the massive cockpit side impact protection walls. The design of the front deflectors was totally original however, having been studied to increase the downforce in a particularly critical area. As well as the usual vertical deflectors, on medium-slow circuits, Ron Dennis' team also used two horizontal pieces, located between the upper and lower suspension wishbone.

McLAREN MERCEDES MP4/12

1997 was also a year of resurrection for team McLaren-Mercedes. After three seasons without a win, poor performances and numerous retirements, Ron Dennis' team finally returned to victory and its traditional F1 role. When, after just one season with the 10 cylinder Peugeot engine, McLaren and Mercedes announced their 'marriage', for the Anglo-German team it was thought that they would be back on the top by 1995. But in modern-day F1, it is not enough just to be called McLaren or Mercedes to guarentee oneself a place in the sun. The ultra-modern technology of today's F1 requires longer periods, careful planning and top-level management. These in turn require two or three seasons before the results start to show. That is why the return of Ron Dennis' team to the victory rostrum, three years after its last Grand Prix win by Ayrton Senna in Australia 1993, increasingly bears the name of Mercedes. Together with the Peugeot engine, the German V10 unit (developed by Mario Illien) is considered to be the most powerful in today's F1 line-up. In its qualifying version, rumours abound of 800 bhp, while the race version should be around 750 bhp. These engine figures, together with good reliability, have enabled McLaren to return amongst the top teams. Although the balance-sheet on the engineering side is in the black, the same cannot be said for the McLaren. The MP4/12 had an acceptable chassis, but its aerodynamics left a lot to be desired.On fast tracks for example, Coulthard and Hakkinen raced with enormous rear wings, a sign of little rear downforce. Furthermore the McLaren was the only '97 car to retain high cockpit sides (introduced last year to protect the head of the driver in case of side impact), which certainly do not help performance. Not to mention the complex bulkheads on the sides of the front wheels, which were greeted with a thumbs-down by many rival designers. The situation in any case will probably improve in 1998 with the arrival within the team of the genial Adrian Newey, the designer whom Ron Dennis lured away from Williams. Newey is probably the best engineer currently in F1. He was responsible for some of the most significant cars of the past few years. When he was still a 'rookie' designer at March-Leyton House, he introduced the idea of a tapered chassis at the front and a raised nose. When he arrived at Williams, he contributed to the development of the unbeatable FW12B, the active-suspension car which dominated the 1992 season with Ni-

1) The same could be said about McLaren as Benetton. In 1997 the team designers limited themselves to just refining the previous year's project, concentrating attention above all on engine development. That is why the aerodynamics remained virtually unchanged and why McLaren was the only top team to maintain the massive cockpit side impact protection walls. The design of the front deflectors was totally original however, having been studied to increase the downforce in a particularly critical area. As well as the usual vertical deflectors, on medium-slow circuits, Ron Dennis' team also used two horizontal pieces, located between the upper and lower suspension wishbone.

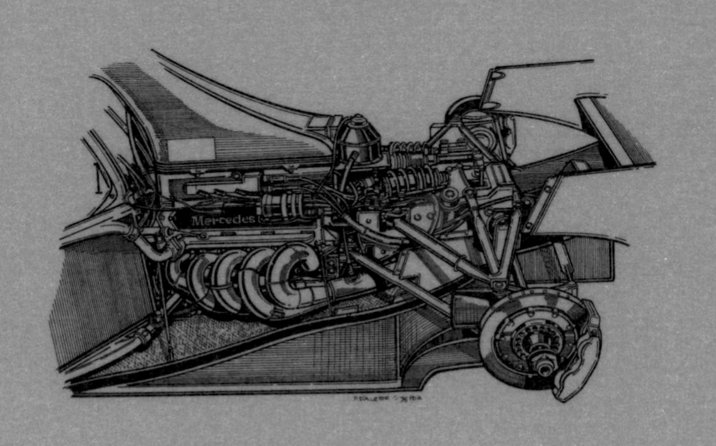
Mercedes

MILD SEVEN
Agip RENAULT
MILD SEVEN
KOREAN AIR
AKAI
EAGLE
GOODYEAR
MILD SEVEN

gel Mansell. Afterwards he designed the world champion cars of Alain Prost (1993) and Damon Hill (1994, together with the constructors' title).
The 1998 season will see Mercedes increasingly involved in F1, both on a financial and a technical-organizational level. The management of the three-pointed star manufacturer are making massive efforts to bring back to Germany a title which has been missing since 1955, the year in which the German Silver Arrows dominated F1 with Fangio and Moss. For this reason, they have agreed to open the purse-strings every time Ron Dennis asks them to. In exchange however, they have obtained one condition; that the team changes its name from 1998 onwards, from its current denomination to Mercedes-McLaren.

---

1) After a year full of ups and downs in 1996, it was thought that the Benetton engineers would have totally revised the design of the car and in 1997 present a completely new model. Instead, nothing of the sort happened. Pat Simonds and Nick Wirth only corrected a few details of the previous year's car, concentrating above all on aerodynamics. Special attention was paid to the design of the bodywork at the rear, where various solutions were seen: the small fins at the start of the year (like Indycars) and the high-speed track version, characterized by a total lack of aerodynamic devices.
2) In order to produce negative lift and downforce on the rear end of the car, Benetton experimented with different types of rear extractors, which however were only useful in certain circumstances. On the mechanical front, attempts were made to resolve the problems of bringing the tyres up to working temperature, by working on the rear suspension. For medium-slow circuits, the triple rear shock absorber seen last year on the B196 was also brought back.

BENETTON RENAULT B197

Only the victory at Hockenheim brought a halt to the downward slide of Benetton. Two years after the departure of Michael Schumacher, the Anglo-Italian team was a shadow of its former self, when it dominated the world championship in the 1994/95 two-year period. In just under two seasons, the revelation of the '90s has gone totally to pieces, and melted away like ice in the sun. In a roundabout way, Ferrari has made a major contribution to Benetton's downfall. First the Anglo-Italian team lost its number 1 driver, the man who contributed more than anything else to its success. Then Rory Byrne and Ross Brawn, the technical brains behind the team and two of the best engineers in F1, switched sides. Finally Flavio Briatore, the team's much-discussed but very skilful manager, left at the end of the season. It is clear that in these conditions, it would have been difficult for anybody to maintain a position of leadership. But for Benetton, the loss was even more serious because the new technical directors, Pat Simonds and Nick Wirth are not at the same level as their predecessors. So as not to complicate things even more, they preferred to develop last year's car rather than design a new one, with results which have been disappointing to say the least.

gel Mansell. Afterwards he designed the world champion cars of Alain Prost (1993) and Damon Hill (1994, together with the constructors' title).

The 1998 season will see Mercedes increasingly involved in F1, both on a financial and a technical-organizational level. The management of the three-pointed star manufacturer are making massive efforts to bring back to Germany a title which has been missing since 1955, the year in which the German Silver Arrows dominated F1 with Fangio and Moss. For this reason, they have agreed to open the purse-strings every time Ron Dennis asks them to. In exchange however, they have obtained one condition; that the team changes its name from 1998 onwards, from its current denomination to Mercedes-McLaren.

BENETTON RENAULT B197

Only the victory at Hockenheim brought a halt to the downward slide of Benetton. Two years after the departure of Michael Schumacher, the Anglo-Italian team was a shadow of its former self, when it dominated the world championship in the 1994/95 two-year period. In just under two seasons, the revelation of the '90s has gone totally to pieces, and melted away like ice in the sun. In a roundabout way, Ferrari has made a major contribution to Benetton's downfall. First the Anglo-Italian team lost its number 1 driver, the man who contributed more than anything else to its success. Then Rory Byrne and Ross Brawn, the technical brains behind the team and two of the best engineers in F1, switched sides. Finally Flavio Briatore, the team's much-discussed but very skilful manager, left at the end of the season. It is clear that in these conditions, it would have been difficult for anybody to maintain a position of leadership. But for Benetton, the loss was even more serious because the new technical directors, Pat Simonds and Nick Wirth are not at the same level as their predecessors. So as not to complicate things even more, they preferred to develop last year's car rather than design a new one, with results which have been disappointing to say the least.

1) After a year full of ups and downs in 1996, it was thought that the Benetton engineers would have totally revised the design of the car and in 1997 present a completely new model. Instead, nothing of the sort happened. Pat Simonds and Nick Wirth only corrected a few details of the previous year's car, concentrating above all on aerodynamics. Special attention was paid to the design of the bodywork at the rear, where various solutions were seen: the small fins at the start of the year (like Indycars) and the high-speed track version, characterized by a total lack of aerodynamic devices.

2) In order to produce negative lift and downforce on the rear end of the car, Benetton experimented with different types of rear extractors, which however were only useful in certain circumstances. On the mechanical front, attempts were made to resolve the problems of bringing the tyres up to working temperature, by working on the rear suspension. For medium-slow circuits, the triple rear shock absorber seen last year on the B196 was also brought back.

MILD SEVEN
Rothmans
elf
Rothmans
RENAULT
MIRAGE
SANYO
SANYO
Rothma
GOODYEAR
SANYO
SONAX
Rothmans

The basic design of the B197 derives from a concept which was developed back in 1992. It is a five-year old design therefore and as such cannot hope to compete with the current cars. Aerodynamically too sensitive to changes in downforce, the 1997 Benetton behaved like Ferraris of previous years; that is to say, it performed very well on certain types of circuit but was a disaster on others. Hockenheim is the shining example. The German track requires a particular set-up, a complex balance which enables the car to be fast on the straights (at speeds of over 300 kph around most of the lap), with sufficient downforce in the medium-slow parts of the Motodrom. In these particular conditions, an old hand of the calibre of Gerhard Berger was perfectly at home, dominating the two qualifying sessions and the race. In all the other circuits, the Anglo-Italian team failed to go better than a few top 6 positions and the occasional podium. Another congenital defect of the B197 was excessive tyre wear, which was also due to imperfect aerodynamics, creating an imbalance especially at the rear.

WILLIAMS FW19-RENAULT

Question: how many Grand Prixs would the Williams have won if Michael Schumacher had been at the wheel of the Anglo-French car and if the team had had the same organization as Ferrari on the track? Answer: a lot more than they have won. Statistics apart, once again (to be exact, for the seventh successive year) the Williams obtained the 'best F1 car' award. To obtain this, the engineers from the Anglo-French team worked in a completely opposite direction to Ferrari.
While at Maranello John Barnard was preparing yet another technological revolution (for the record, the British designer produced four different cars in four years), at Grove progress was being made by following methods which had been consolidated over the years - developing and refining a basic project step by step without overhauling it completely, and improving each time the small details which make all the difference and enable precious tenths of a second to be gained. In view of this consideration, we could say that the 1997 car, called FW19, is the logical development of a project which came to light in 1994.
This year, the attention of engineers under the guidance of Patrick Head was in particular con-

1) If we observe the various Williams cars of the past few years, minimal differences can be noted between one car and another. This year's FW19 for example, was a logical development of the 1996 car, which in turn derived from the previous year's version. These operating methods allowed the team to remain always on the crest of the wave, constantly refining the basic design project, which was good right from the start, without having to modify it drastically year after year, the exact opposite to what Barnard was doing at Ferrari.
2) In the diagrams viewed from above and the cross-section drawing of the FW19, one can see the major differences between the '96 and the '97 versions. The main modifications are all concentrated in the central part of the car. The sides of the FW19 are considerably smaller and shorter, thanks to the use of radiant masses with small dimensions and the capacity of the 10 cylinder Renault engine to work at working temperatures which were considerably higher than most of the opposition. It is also to be noted that the Williams was the first car to abandon the additional flaps, mounted in front of the driving wheels and, together with Jordan, the first team to give up on the fashion of rounded air intakes, separated from the car body.

The basic design of the B197 derives from a concept which was developed back in 1992. It is a five-year old design therefore and as such cannot hope to compete with the current cars. Aerodynamically too sensitive to changes in downforce, the 1997 Benetton behaved like Ferraris of previous years; that is to say, it performed very well on certain types of circuit but was a disaster on others. Hockenheim is the shining example. The German track requires a particular set-up, a complex balance which enables the car to be fast on the straights (at speeds of over 300 kph around most of the lap), with sufficient downforce in the medium-slow parts of the Motodrom. In these particular conditions, an old hand of the calibre of Gerhard Berger was perfectly at home, dominating the two qualifying sessions and the race. In all the other circuits, the Anglo-Italian team failed to go better than a few top 6 positions and the occasional podium. Another congenital defect of the B197 was excessive tyre wear, which was also due to imperfect aerodynamics, creating an imbalance especially at the rear.

WILLIAMS FW19-RENAULT

Question: how many Grand Prixs would the Williams have won if Michael Schumacher had been at the wheel of the Anglo-French car and if the team had had the same organization as Ferrari on the track? Answer: a lot more than they have won. Statistics apart, once again (to be exact, for the seventh successive year) the Williams obtained the 'best F1 car' award. To obtain this, the engineers from the Anglo-French team worked in a completely opposite direction to Ferrari.

While at Maranello John Barnard was preparing yet another technological revolution (for the record, the British designer produced four different cars in four years), at Grove progress was being made by following methods which had been consolidated over the years - developing and refining a basic project step by step without overhauling it completely, and improving each time the small details which make all the difference and enable precious tenths of a second to be gained. In view of this consideration, we could say that the 1997 car, called FW19, is the logical development of a project which came to light in 1994.

This year, the attention of engineers under the guidance of Patrick Head was in particular con-

1) If we observe the various Williams cars of the past few years, minimal differences can be noted between one car and another. This year's FW19 for example, was a logical development of the 1996 car, which in turn derived from the previous year's version. These operating methods allowed the team to remain always on the crest of the wave, constantly refining the basic design project, which was good right from the start, without having to modify it drastically year after year, the exact opposite to what Barnard was doing at Ferrari.

2) In the diagrams viewed from above and the cross-section drawing of the FW19, one can see the major differences between the '96 and the '97 versions. The main modifications are all concentrated in the central part of the car. The sides of the FW19 are considerably smaller and shorter, thanks to the use of radiant masses with small dimensions and the capacity of the 10 cylinder Renault engine to work at working temperatures which were considerably higher than most of the opposition. It is also to be noted that the Williams was the first car to abandon the additional flaps, mounted in front of the driving wheels and, together with Jordan, the first team to give up on the fashion of rounded air intakes, separated from the car body.

Rothmans
Castrol
RENAULT
Rothmans
elf
Rothmans
Castrol
RENAULT
Rothmans
HYPE
SONAX
GOODYEAR
Rothmans

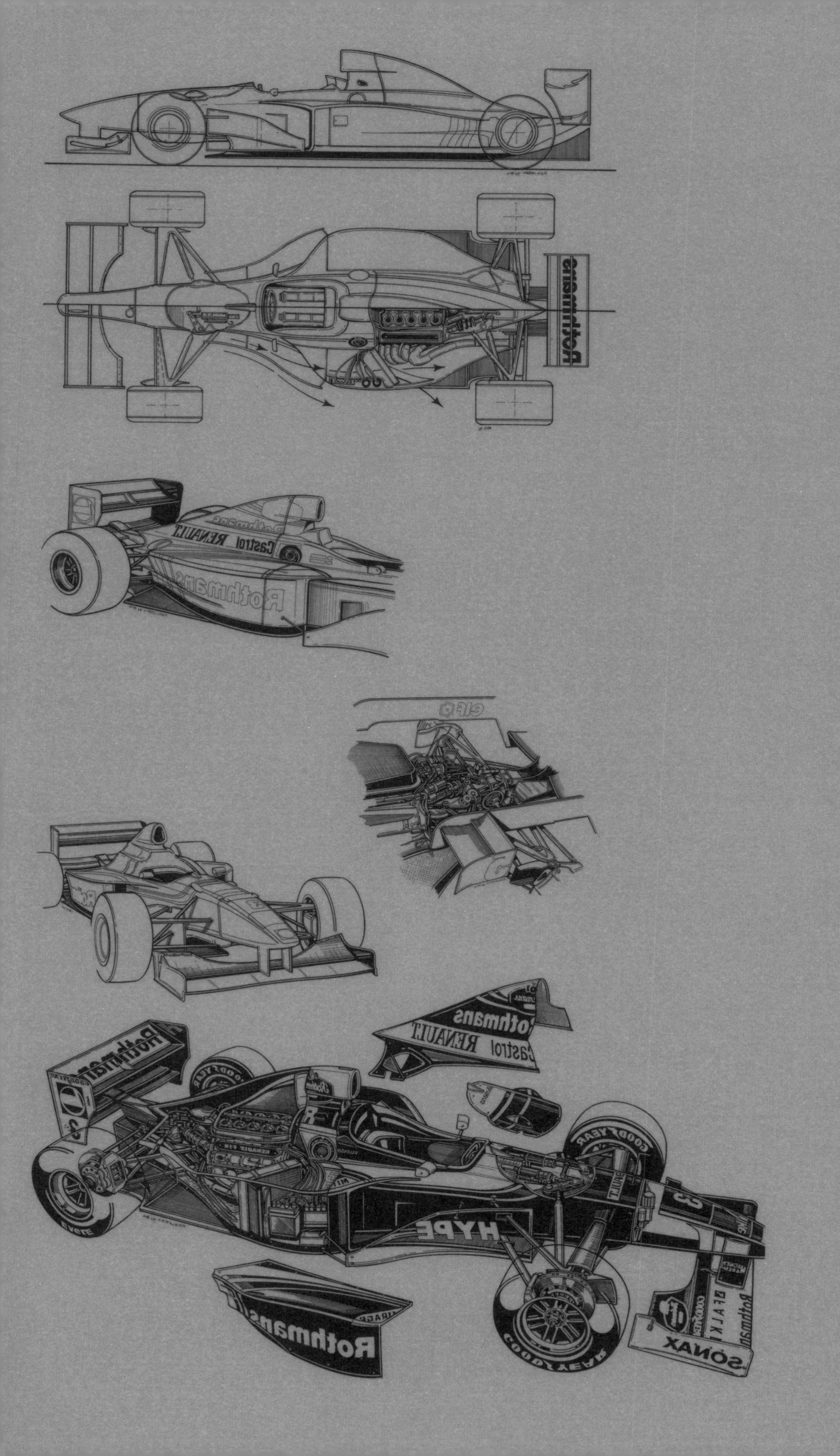

centrated on aerodynamics, one of those sectors where a certain difference between the cars can still be found. A scale model of the Williams FW19 underwent lengthy tests in the team's new wind tunnel (which can house 1:2 scale models) and the final result was a substantial reduction of the size of the car. The dimensions of the FW19 were so much smaller than those of the FW18 that many people defined the new Williams as the only real 'new' car of the 1997 season. All the other teams, more or less, ended up by copying all the good features of the 1996 championship-winning car, adapting their cars to the different engines used.
To get an idea of the basis behind this theory, it is only necessary to compare the lateral dimensions of the FW19 with those of the other F1 cars. The dimensions of the sides of Villeneuve's and Frentzen's cars are 15-20% smaller than those of the cars of other teams. This is due to accurate studies carried out on internal fluidodynamics and the miniaturization of masses by Renault. The French manufacturer (which retired from Grand Prixs at the end of 1997), as well as perfecting the cooling of its engine, also debuted a brand-new 10 cylinder unit (called RS9) which was more compact and lighter than the previous RS8 and which had higher revs (500) and naturally dozens of additional horse power. Other modifications produced by Williams in 1997 were the new engine air intakes (rounded and separate from the chassis) and faired suspensions, which have now become a key development for all F1 designers.
But there are still several negative aspects in the technical balance-sheet of the season which has just concluded: first of all a slowing down in car development half-way through the season, due to Adrian Newey leaving the team. After years of collaboration with Patrick Head, Adrian Newey was tempted by McLaren and left the Grove-based team at the start of the season. Williams, which in the past had been used to dealing out the final blow to its world championship rivals when the Circus arrived at the fast tracks, started to have problems on those circuits where it was favourite for victory. Starting from the end of August, there was however some development work done on the cars of Villeneuve and Frentzen.

centrated on aerodynamics, one of those sectors where a certain difference between the cars can still be found. A scale model of the Williams FW19 underwent lengthy tests in the team's new wind tunnel (which can house 1:2 scale models) and the final result was a substantial reduction of the size of the car. The dimensions of the FW19 were so much smaller than those of the FW18 that many people defined the new Williams as the only real 'new' car of the 1997 season. All the other teams, more or less, ended up by copying all the good features of the 1996 championship-winning car, adapting their cars to the different engines used.
To get an idea of the basis behind this theory, it is only necessary to compare the lateral dimensions of the FW19 with those of the other F1 cars. The dimensions of the sides of Villeneuve's and Frentzen's cars are 15-20% smaller than those of the cars of other teams. This is due to accurate studies carried out on internal fluidodynamics and the miniaturization of masses by Renault. The French manufacturer (which retired from Grand Prixs at the end of 1997), as well as perfecting the cooling of its engine, also debuted a brand-new 10 cylinder unit (called RS9) which was more compact and lighter than the previous RS8 and which had higher revs (500) and naturally dozens of additional horse power. Other modifications produced by Williams in 1997 were the new engine air intakes (rounded and separate from the chassis) and faired suspensions, which have now become a key development for all F1 designers.
But there are still several negative aspects in the technical balance-sheet of the season which has just concluded: first of all a slowing down in car development half-way through the season, due to Adrian Newey leaving the team. After years of collaboration with Patrick Head, Adrian Newey was tempted by McLaren and left the Grove-based team at the start of the season. Williams, which in the past had been used to dealing out the final blow to its world championship rivals when the Circus arrived at the fast tracks, started to have problems on those circuits where it was favourite for victory. Starting from the end of August, there was however some development work done on the cars of Villeneuve and Frentzen.

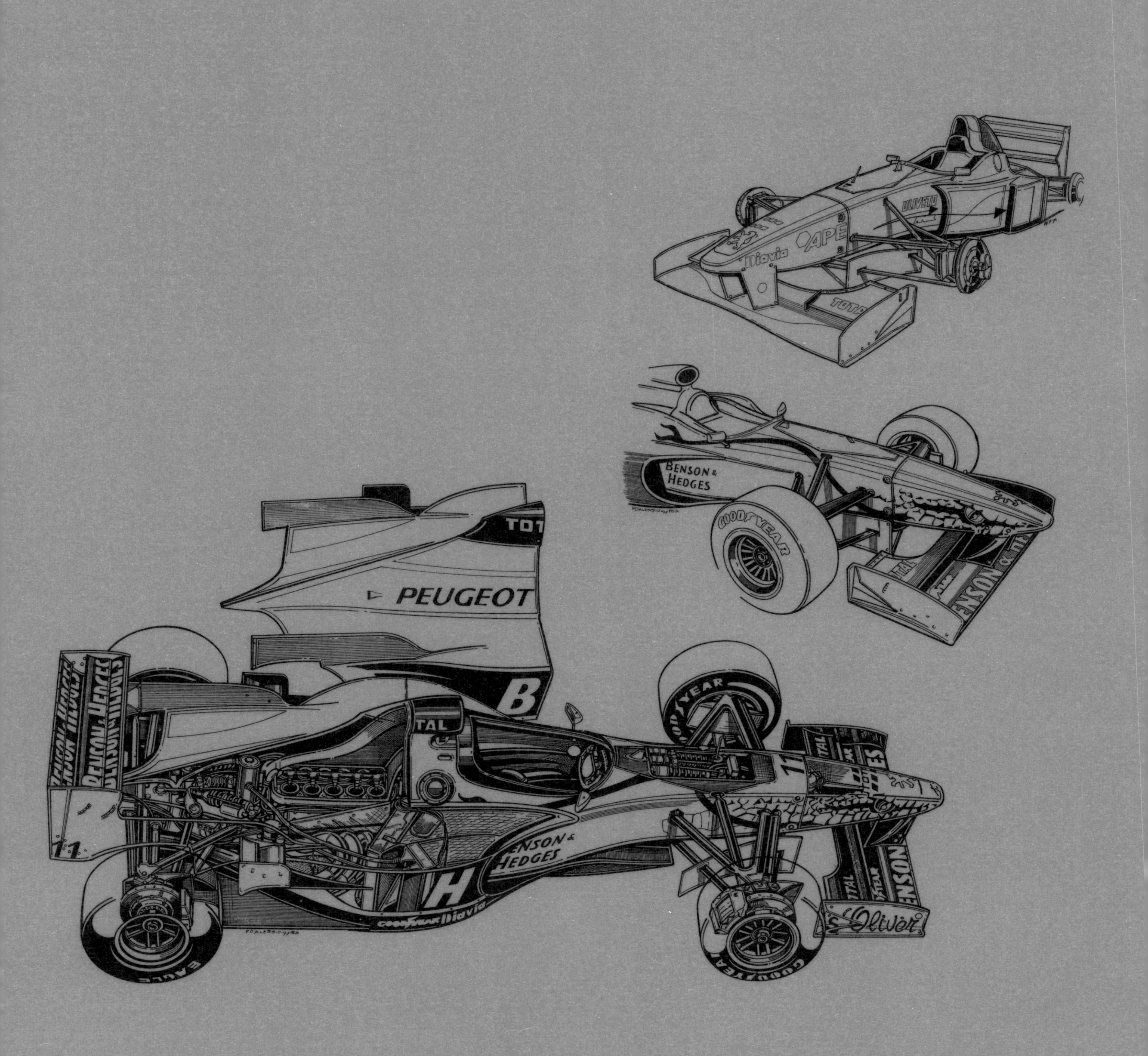

PEUGEOT
BENSON & HEDGES
BENSON & HEDGES
GOODYEAR

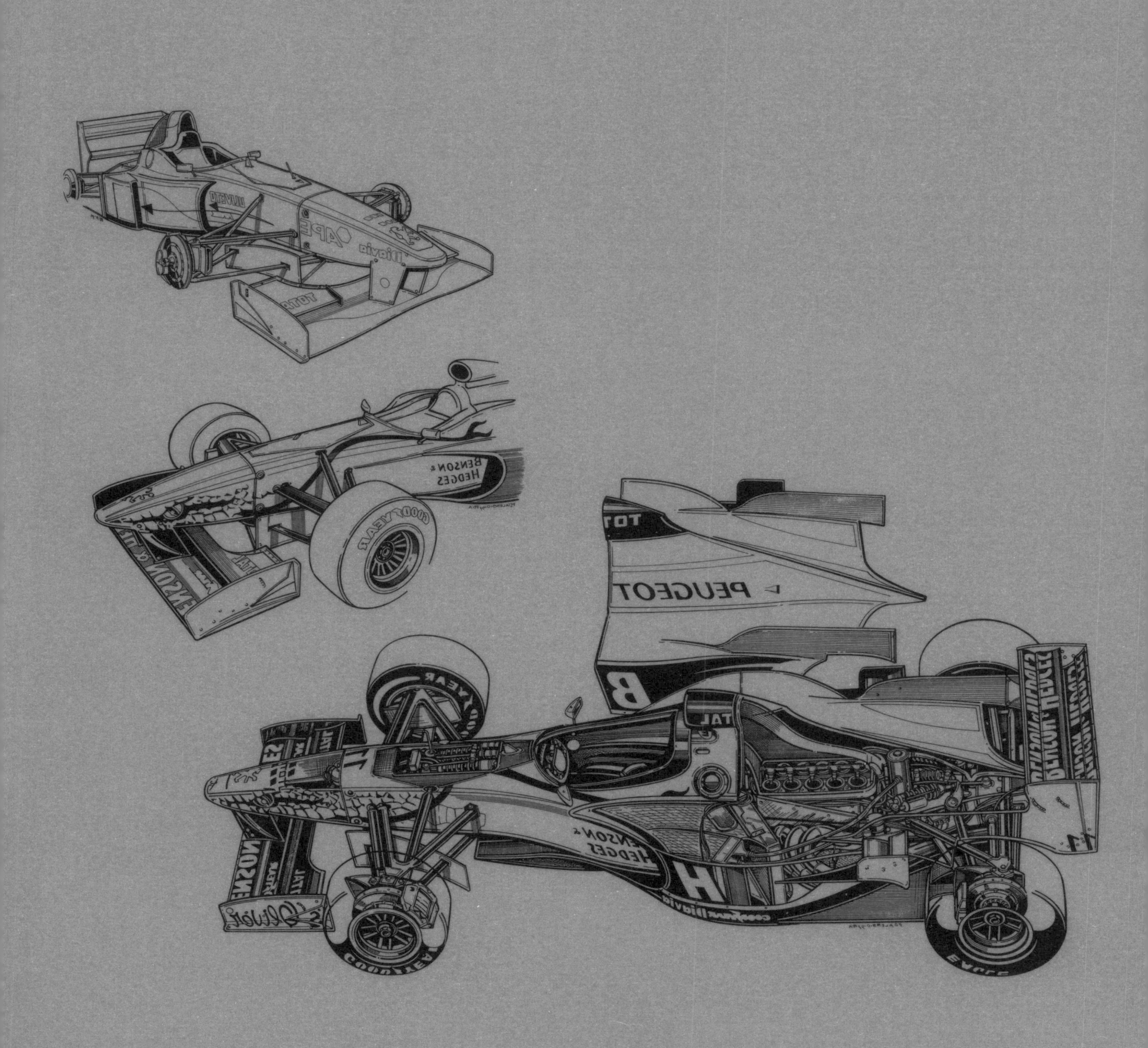
BENSON & HEDGES
PEUGEOT

JORDAN PEUGEOT 197

Eddie Jordan is the prototype of a 1990s F1 team manager - open-minded, astute and far-sighted. 1997 was a crucial year for his team: were it to have disputed an excellent season, the Anglo-Irish team would have carved out a space for itself amongst the top teams. Otherwise, it would have lost the support of Peugeot and the backing of some big name sponsors. Clearly the only solution available for the resourceful Jordan was the former. To remain amongst the big names in F1, the Irish team manager did not hesitate to make a major effort, strengthening above all the technical side of things, the sector where it was the weakest. As hoped for, the results arrived and with them, the recognition of the rest of the F1 world, which promoted his team to the 'premier league'; even Patrick Head, Frank Williams' partner (as well as engineering brains behind the team since 1978) was heard to say that 'after the Williams, the best car of 1997 is the Jordan'. Quite a compliment seeing how Head, as well as being considered one of the geniuses of the category, is also noted for his few words and his presumptuousness. Head's compliments were in particular addressed to Gary Anderson, Jordan's brilliant designer, who having rid himself of the tag of chief mechanic, has now taken on (successfully) the job of engineer.
His 197 is a classic example of 'Made in England' design pragmatism. A simple, compact car, easy to set up and suitable for all types of circuit. The exact opposite to the designs of some of his more famous colleagues. A 'simple' car, but not without some original points, starting with its aerodynamic configuration. In 1997 Anderson abandoned last year's design which was characterized by the presence of sides with a twin air intake. In their place, he introduced medium-length lateral pontoons and the distribution of radiant masses within the sides. This was a major piece of work, seeing as this area is one of those which greatly conditions the functioning of a modern-day F1 car. A correct design of the lateral pontoons and good internal fluido-dynamics, as well as improving the aerodynamics, in fact allow the engine to work under its best conditions and at the right working temperatures. Regarding engines, according to those who know, the 1997 version of the 10 cylinder Peugeot unit was probably the one with the best overall performance, together with the V10 Mercedes. A reliable engine, one which with a certain regularity, could aspire to victory. Next year however, the French engine manufacturer will be changing team. The unit designed by Jean-Pierre Boudy will switch to Prost (to form an all-French team), while Eddie Jordan will have a supply of Honda-Mugen engines. The Japanese manufacturer is progressing well on the engine front and wants to return to the top as soon as possible, after having dominated F1 between 1986 and 1991.

1) Simple construction, reduced dimensions, reliability and good aerodynamics were the winning features of the 1997 Jordan. The team has made giant strides over the past 12 months thanks also to the excellent qualities of the 10 cylinder Peugeot engine, unanimously considered to be one of the most powerful around. Unlike the 1996 car (characterized by sides with twin air intakes), the 197 is more simple, but with a number of significant original features, such as the rounded shape of the sides or that of the engine air intake, similar to solutions used by BRM and March in the 1970s.

JORDAN PEUGEOT 197

Eddie Jordan is the prototype of a 1990s F1 team manager - open-minded, astute and far-sighted. 1997 was a crucial year for his team: were it to have disputed an excellent season, the Anglo-Irish team would have carved out a space for itself amongst the top teams. Otherwise, it would have lost the support of Peugeot and the backing of some big name sponsors. Clearly the only solution available for the resourceful Jordan was the former. To remain amongst the big names in F1, the Irish team manager did not hesitate to make a major effort, strengthening above all the technical side of things, the sector where it was the weakest. As hoped for, the results arrived and with them, the recognition of the rest of the F1 world, which promoted his team to the 'premier league'; even Patrick Head, Frank Williams' partner (as well as engineering brains behind the team since 1978) was heard to say that 'after the Williams, the best car of 1997 is the Jordan'. Quite a compliment seeing how Head, as well as being considered one of the geniuses of the category, is also noted for his few words and his presumptuousness. Head's compliments were in particular addressed to Gary Anderson, Jordan's brilliant designer, who having rid himself of the tag of chief mechanic, has now taken on (successfully) the job of engineer.

His 197 is a classic example of 'Made in England' design pragmatism. A simple, compact car, easy to set up and suitable for all types of circuit. The exact opposite to the designs of some of his more famous colleagues. A 'simple' car, but not without some original points, starting with its aerodynamic configuration. In 1997 Anderson abandoned last year's design which was characterized by the presence of sides with a twin air intake. In their place, he introduced medium-length lateral pontoons and the distribution of radiant masses within the sides. This was a major piece of work, seeing as this area is one of those which greatly conditions the functioning of a modern-day F1 car. A correct design of the lateral pontoons and good internal fluido-dynamics, as well as improving the aerodynamics, in fact allow the engine to work under its best conditions and at the right working temperatures. Regarding engines, according to those who know, the 1997 version of the 10 cylinder Peugeot unit was probably the one with the best overall performance, together with the V10 Mercedes. A reliable engine, one which with a certain regularity, could aspire to victory. Next year however, the French engine manufacturer will be changing team. The unit designed by Jean-Pierre Boudy will switch to Prost (to form an all-French team), while Eddie Jordan will have a supply of Honda-Mugen engines. The Japanese manufacturer is progressing well on the engine front and wants to return to the top as soon as possible, after having dominated F1 between 1986 and 1991.

1) Simple construction, reduced dimensions, reliability and good aerodynamics were the winning features of the 1997 Jordan. The team has made giant strides over the past 12 months thanks also to the excellent qualities of the 10 cylinder Peugeot engine, unanimously considered to be one of the most powerful around. Unlike the 1996 car (characterized by sides with twin air intakes), the 197 is more simple, but with a number of significant original features, such as the rounded shape of the sides or that of the engine air intake, similar to solutions used by BRM and March in the 1970s.

F1 '97

Australian GP

1990 N. Piquet
1991 A. Senna
1992 G. Berger
1993 A. Senna
1994 N. Mansell
1995 D. Hill
1996 D. Hill

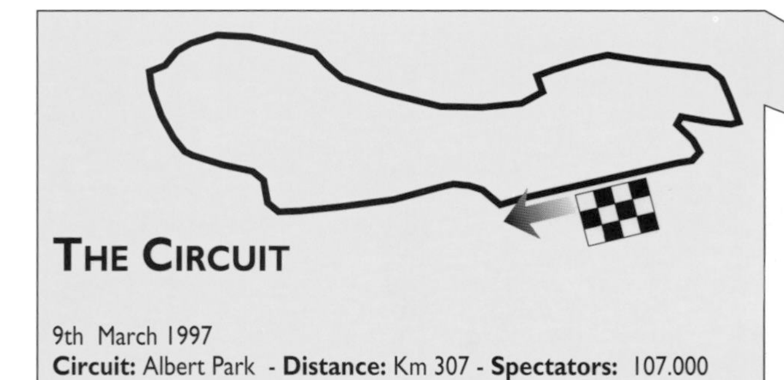

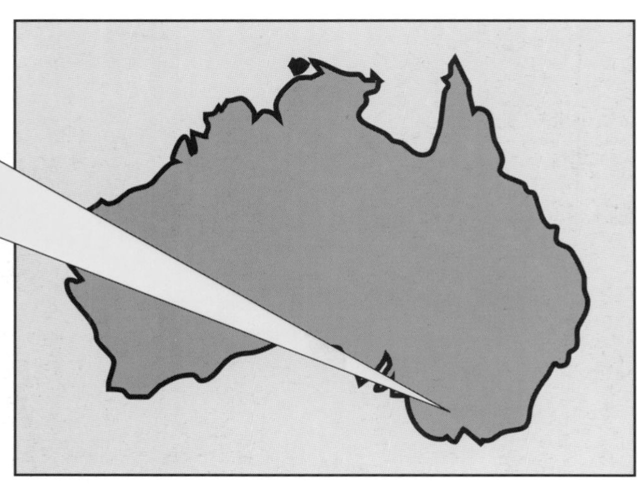

The Circuit

9th March 1997
Circuit: Albert Park - **Distance:** Km 307 - **Spectators:** 107.000

Starting grid

Pos	Left	Right
1	J. Villeneuve Williams 1'29"369 (213,577)	H. H. Frentzen Williams 1'31"123 (209,466)
2	M. Schumacher Ferrari 1'31"472 (208,667)	D. Coulthard McLaren 1'31"531 (208,533)
3	E. Irvine Ferrari 1'31"881 (207,738)	M. Hakkinen McLaren 1'31"971 (207,535)
4	J. Herbert Sauber 1'32"287 (206,824)	J. Alesi Benetton 1'32"593 (206,141)
5	O. Panis Prost 1'32"642 (206,032)	G. Berger Benetton 1'32"870 (205,526)
6	R. Barrichello Stewart 1'33"075 (205,073)	R. Schumacher Jordan 1'33"130 (204,952)
7	N. Larini Sauber 1'33"327 (204,520)	G. Fisichella Jordan 1'33"552 (204,028)
8	U. Katayama Minardi 1'33"798 (203,493)	S. Nakano Prost 1'33"989 (203,079)
9	J. Trulli Minardi 1'34"120 (202,796)	M. Salo Tyrrell 1'34"229 (202,562)
10	J. Magnussen Stewart 1'34"623 (201,718)	D. Hill Arrows 1'34"806 (201,329)
11	J. Verstappen Tyrrell 1'34"943 (201,039)	P. Diniz Arrows 1'35"972 (198,883)
	V. Sospiri Lola 1'40"972 (189,035)	R. Rosset Lola 1'42"086 (186,972)

Lightning struck at Melbourne in the form of Jacques Villeneuve. The Canadian driver was favourite for the 1997 title and he knew it.
He came to Melbourne, the Albert Park circuit which one year before had marked his official debut in F1, and dominated qualifying.
The front row of the grid was all-Williams, but Frentzen in second place was exactly 1.754" behind - more than three-tenths of a second per kilometre down on the Canadian - an absolutely incredible performance!
More news from qualifying: Ferrari took to the track with its well-tested F310B and Schumacher and Irvine were third and fifth fastest, with the McLarens of Coulthard and Hakinen ahead of and behind the Irish driver. But the gap between Villeneuve and these four was between 2.1" and 2.6" ...
It was logical to expect a triumphant cavalcade for Villeneuve and Williams but it wasn't to be. At the first curve Irvine, who had rocketed away from the third row, hit the Williams of Villeneuve, who had slipped his clutch and had started badly. Herbert's Sauber was also involved in the incident. They all retired on the spot, but at least their fate was less embarassing than that of Hill, who had struggled to twentieth on the grid in qualifying and whose throttle cable broke during the warm-up lap.
At the end of lap 1, Frentzen had the race in the bag, but then his Williams began to have brake problems.
The German was overtaken by Coulthard's McLaren and Schumacher's Ferrari, now first and second. Michael had to pit for a splash of fuel, leaving the Williams driver in second place.
But he then lost that position two laps from the end when his brakes seized, sending him into the gravel.
Two McLarens on the podium: first Coulthard and third Hakkinen, separated by Schumacher's Ferrari.
Forty-two years after the last world title conquered with Fangio, the silver colour of Mercedes had triumphed again in F1.

Results

	Driver	Car	Avg.	Gap
1	D. Coulthard	McLaren	203.926	
2	M. Schumacher	Ferrari	203.176	20"046
3	M. Hakkinen	McLaren	203.096	22"177
4	G. Berger	Benetton	203.072	22"841
5	O. Panis	Prost	201.686	1'00"308
6	N. Narini	Sauber	200.381	1'36"040
7	S. Nakano	Prost	195.353	2 laps
8	H.H. Franntzen	Williams	193.904	3 laps
9	J. Trulli	Minardi	193.210	3 laps
10	P. Diniz	Arrows	188.392	4 laps

Retirements

Driver	Car	Lap	Reason
D. Hill	Arrows	0	Accelerator
J. Herbert	Sauber	0	Accident
J. Villeneuve	Williams	0	Accident
E. Irvine	Ferrari	0	Accident
R. Schumacher	Jordan	1	Axle-shaft
J. Verstappen	Tyrrell	2	Crashed
G. Fisichella	Jordan	14	Spunn off
U. Katayama	Minardi	32	Start
J. Alesi	Benetton	34	Engine
J. Magnussen	Stewart	36	Suspension
M. Salo	Tyrrel	42	Engine
R. Barrichello	Stewart	49	Engine

Topspeed

Driver	Max.
Villeneuve	291.100
Alesi	289.500
Hakkinen	289.500
Frentzen	287.200
Larini	287.200
Coulthard	287.200
Herbert	284.900
Panis	284.200
Magnussen	284.200
Nakano	283.400
Barrichello	283.400
Fisichella	282.700
Irvine	282.700
M. Schumacher	281.900
Verstappen	281.900
Diniz	281.900
Katayama	281.900

Traditional start-of-season photograph for the 24 F1 drivers. Amongst them, several new faces. For example, the four drivers confirming Italy's increasing presence in F1. From left to right, Fisichella, Larini and the two 'rookies' Trulli and Sospiri. The latter made his debut in the number 24 Lola, while the number 25 was given to the Brazilian, Rosset. After an incident-packed start which eliminated Villeneuve, Irvine and Herbert, the Grand Prix saw the victory of David Coulthard, here celebrating with team owner Ron Dennis. This was Coulthard's second victory in F1, while for McLaren it was their 105th, three years after the last one in 1993. That also came in Australia, but in Adelaide, and with Ayrton Senna at the wheel. Mercedes hadn't won a Grand Prix since 1955 ...

Brazilian GP

1990 A. Prost
1991 A. Senna
1992 N. Mansell
1993 A. Senna
1994 M. Schumacher
1995 M. Schumacher
1996 D. Hill

The Circuit

30th March 1997
Circuit: Interlagos
Distance: Km 309
Spectators: 55.000

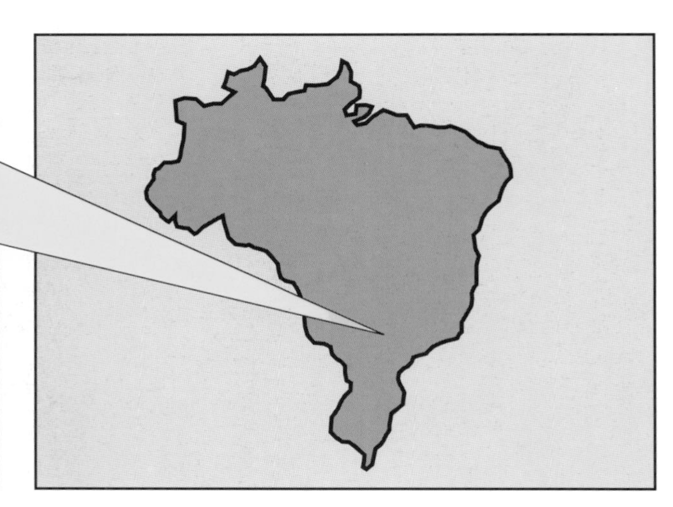

Starting Grid

Row		
1	**J. Villeneuve** Williams 1'16"004 (203,295)	**M. Schumacher** Ferrari 1'16"594 (201,729)
2	**G. Berger** Benetton 1'16"644 (201,597)	**M. Hakkinen** McLaren 1'16"692 (201,471)
3	**O. Panis** Prost 1'16"756 (201,303)	**J. Alesi** Benetton 1'16"757 (201,300)
4	**G. Fisichella** Jordan 1'16"912 (200,895)	**H. H. Frentzen** Williams 1'16"924 (200,863)
5	**D. Hill** Arrows 1'17"090 (200,431)	**R. Schumacher** Jordan 1'17"175 (200,210)
6	**R. Barrichello** Stewart 1'17"259 (199,992)	**D. Coulthard** McLaren 1'17"262 (199,984)
7	**J. Herbert** Sauber 1'17"409 (199,605)	**E. Irvine** Ferrari 1'17"527 (199,301)
8	**S. Nakano** Prost 1'17"999 (198,095)	**P. Diniz** Arrows 1'18"095 (197,851)
9	**J. Trulli** Minardi 1'18"336 (197,243)	**U. Katayama** Minardi 1'18"557 (196,688)
10	**N. Larini** Sauber 1'18"644 (196,470)	**J. Magnussen** Stewart 1'18"773 (196,148)
11	**J. Verstappen** Tyrrell 1'18"885 (195,870)	**M. Salo** Tyrrell 1'19"274 (194,909)

It was only the second round and the world championship was already heading for a showdown. "With this Williams - declared Villeneuve - I can win easily ... as long as Irvine stays out of my way". Joking apart, the Canadian dominated qualifying. The Williams appeared to have an extra gear at Interlagos, a 'real' race-circuit. It clearly seemed to have more gears than the Ferrari, which was in difficulty on the fast curves requiring lots of downforce but not much in the way of aerodynamics. Even with this handicap, Schumacher pulled out all the stops and set a fast lap which earned him the front row, despite being more than half-a-second down on Villeneuve. Behind the Ferrari was Berger's Benetton and Hakkinen's McLaren. Then came the surprising Prost of Panis ahead of Alesi's Benetton and Fisichella in the Jordan. Frentzen was only eighth, while Hill moved up to ninth in the Arrows.
The race got underway with a surprise for Villeneuve. Schumacher got the better start and led into the Senna curve. In his attempt to get the better of the Ferrari, Villeneuve went off and returned to the track ninth. Just as well that many others went off at the same point and that Barrichello's Stewart was stopped on the starting-grid.
The race was interrupted and they had to start all over again. Schumacher got the better start once again, but this time Villeneuve stayed cool. He slotted in behind the Ferrari and at the end of the first lap powered past Schumacher in front of the pits. His only worry was a not entirely perfect final set of tyres, which lost him vital seconds to a hard-charging Berger. The Austrian finished second ahead of Panis in the Prost. With this victory, Villeneuve moved into the lead of the championship on level points with Coulthard.
Schumacher was a disappointed fifth and was beaten on the road by Hakkinen in the McLaren.

Results

	Driver	Car	Avg.	Gap
1	J. Villeneuve	Williams	192.906	
2	G. Berger	Benetton	192.766	4"190
3	O. Panis	Prost	192.377	15"870
4	M. Hakkinen	McLaren	191.808	33"033
5	M. Schumacher	Ferrari	191.784	33"731
6	J. Alesi	Benetton	191.775	34"020
7	J. Herbert	Sauber	191.218	50"912
8	G. Fisichella	Jordan	190.899	1'00"639
9	H.H. Frentzen	Williams	190.416	1'15"402
10	D. Coulthard	McLaren	190.101	1 lap
11	N. Larini	Sauber	189.876	1 lap
12	J. Trulli	Minardi	188.685	1 lap
13	M. Salo	Tyrrell	187.831	1 lap
14	S. Nakano	Prost	187.681	1 lap
15	J. Verstappen	Tyrrell	187.258	2 laps
16	E. Irvine	Ferrari	187.107	2 laps
17	D. Hill	Arrows	189.126	4 laps

Retirements

Driver	Car	Lap	Reason
P. Diniz	Arrows	15	Spunn off
R. Barrichello	Stewart	16	Suspension
R. Schumacher	Jordan	52	Engine

Topspeed

Driver	Max.
Villeneuve	299.100
Alesi	299.100
Fisichella	298.300
Frentzen	297.500
Coulthard	296.700
R. Schumacher	296.700
Berger	296.700
Nakano	295.800
Hakkinen	295.000
Panis	295.000
M. Schumacher	294.200
Irvine	294.200
Barrichello	293.400
Veerstappen	293.400
Herbert	292.600
Larini	291.100
Diniz	291.100

Triumph for Jacques Villeneuve, who scored his first win of the season at Interlagos, his fifth overall in 18 races in F1. It was a historic victory for the Canadian: race win, pole position and fastest lap, the first time he had scored a 'hat-trick' in F1. Less joy however for the Arrows team. The second race of the season for the 1996 champion Damon Hill was a disaster: he was classified 17th, 4 laps behind the winner but failed to finish the race. The second Arrows of Diniz stopped after a spin.

ARGENTINE GP

1995 D. Hill
1996 D. Hill

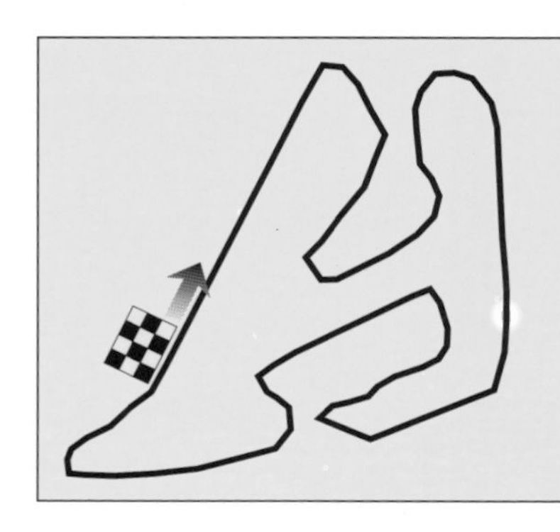

THE CIRCUIT

13th April 1997
Circuit: Oscar A.Galvez
Distance: Km 306
Spectators: 70.000

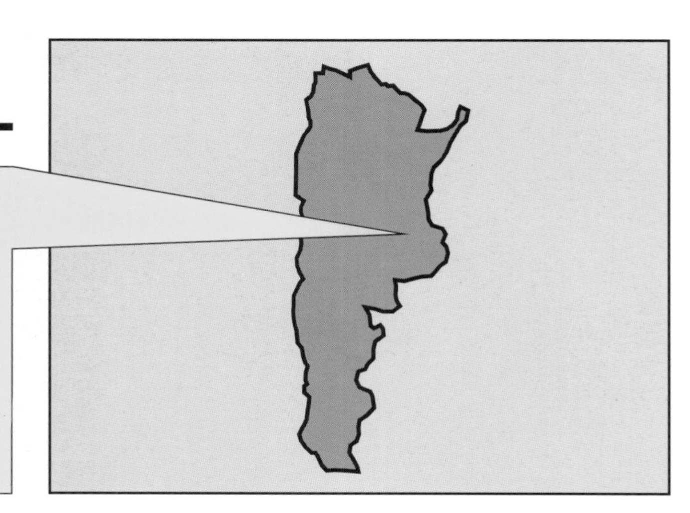

STARTING GRID

Pos	Driver	Car	Time	Speed
1	J. Villeneuve	Williams	1'24"473	(181,507)
	H. H. Frentzen	Williams	1'25"271	(179,808)
2	O. Panis	Prost	1'25"491	(179,345)
	M. Schumacher	Ferrari	1'25"773	(178,756)
3	R. Barrichello	Stewart	1'25"942	(178,404)
	R. Schumacher	Jordan	1'26"218	(177,833)
4	E. Irvine	Ferrari	1'26"327	(177,608)
	J. Herbert	Sauber	1'26"564	(177,122)
5	G. Fisichella	Jordan	1'26"619	(177,010)
	D. Coulthard	McLaren	1'26"799	(176,643)
6	J. Alesi	Benetton	1'27"076	(176,081)
	G. Berger	Benetton	1'27"259	(175,711)
7	D. Hill	Arrows	1'27"281	(175,667)
	N. Larini	Sauber	1'27"690	(174,848)
8	J. Magnussen	Stewart	1'28"035	(174,163)
	J. Verstappen	Tyrrell	1'28"094	(174,046)
9	M. Hakkinen	McLaren	1'28"135	(173,965)
	J. Trulli	Minardi	1'28"160	(173,916)
10	M. Salo	Tyrrell	1'28"224	(173,789)
	S. Nakano	Prost	1'28"366	(173,510)
11	U. Katayama	Minardi	1'28"413	(173,418)
	P. Diniz	Arrows	1'28"969	(172,334)

Buenos Aires was still in the height of summer, which in this part of the world lasts from April to late autumn. But when Jacques Villeneuve got off the plane, it was clear that his physical condition was not in harmony with the sunny Buenos Aires weather. The Canadian was suffering from a stomach infection and after Saturday qualifying he had to undergo medical treatment. This didn't affect his performance however. Looking paler than ever, he went out and set his third pole position in three races, winning his second GP of the year and moved into the lead of the championship with 20 points, twice as many as Coulthard, winner of the first round but out of the points in the other two.
The race was all about Villeneuve. In the similar Williams, Frentzen was totally overshadowed by the Canadian. He also was not in the best physical condition but that did not justify the eight-tenths of a second which separated his second place on the grid from the pole. In the race, he lost sixth gear and ended up on the 'desparacido' list.
Even the Ferraris could do little against the Villeneuve/Williams combination. Schumacher was fourth in qualifying, slower than Panis and his Prost, which was lying second in the race before hydraulics problems caused him to retire. The German had a worse race. At the start he made wheel contact with Panis, bending the Frenchman's suspension. A few metres later, he collided with the Stewart of Barrichello, who managed to make it back to the pits while the German parked his number 5 Ferrari on the grass.
At the end of a Grand Prix which had been livened up by the entrance of the safety-car (the first time this year), Villeneuve won by less than a second from Irvine, who had made up ground on the Canadian more due to the latter's physical problems than to the Ferrari's actual performance. Third, after a clash with his teammate Fisichella, who was ahead of him at the time, was Ralf Schumacher with the first F1 points of his career.

RESULTS

	DRIVER	CAR	AVG.	GAP
1	J. Villeneuve	Williams	164.155	
2	E. Irvine	Ferrari	164.131	"979
3	R. Schumacher	Jordan	163.860	12"089
4	J. Herbert	Sauber	163.428	29"919
5	M. Hakkinen	McLaren	163.417	30"351
6	G. Berger	Benetton	163.392	31"393
7	J. Alesi	Benetton	163.031	46"359
8	M. Salo	Tyrrell	160.518	1 lap
9	J. Trulli	Minardi	159.812	1 lap
10	J. Magnussen	Stewart	158.659	6 laps

RETIREMENTS

DRIVER	CAR	LAP	RAISON
D. Coulthard	McLaren	1	Accident
M. Schumacher	Ferrari	1	Accident
H.H. Frentzen	Williams	5	Gear
O. Panis	Prost	18	Electrical fault
R. Barrichello	Stewart	24	Accelerator
G. Fisichella	Jordan	24	Accident
D. Hill	Arrows	33	Hydraulic circuit
U. Katayama	Minardi	37	Crashed
J. Verstappen	Tyrrell	43	Engine
S. Nakano	Prost	49	Hydraulic circuit
P. Diniz	Arrows	50	Gear
N. Larini	Sauber	63	Spunn off

TOPSPEED

DRIVER	MAX.
Villeneuve	250.000
R. Schumacher	248.200
Frentzen	248.200
Fisichella	247.700
Coulthard	247.100
Berger	246.500
Alesi	246.000
Larini	246.000
M. Schumacher	244.800
Hakkinen	244.800
Panis	244.800
Herbert	244.300
Nakano	243.200
Irvine	242.600
Magnussen	241.600
Diniz	241.000
Barrichello	240.500

A second successive victory for Villeneuve, here spraying champagne on the podium together with Irvine and Ralf Schumacher, second and third respectively.
The Canadian now led the world championship on 20 points: double the total of Berger and Coulthard. Another poor result for the other Williams driver, Frentzen. Not even a walk around the circuit with his engineers helped him much in the race. No points in the race for Michael Schumacher, who was involved in a collision which brought his Ferrari to a halt immediately after the start and forced him to walk back to the pits.

San Marino GP

1990 R. Patrese
1991 A. Senna
1992 N. Mansell
1993 A. Prost
1994 M. Schumacher
1995 D. Hill
1996 D. Hill

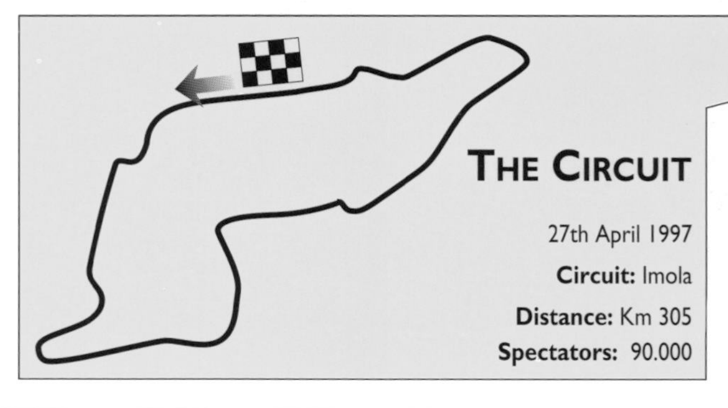

The Circuit

27th April 1997
Circuit: Imola
Distance: Km 305
Spectators: 90.000

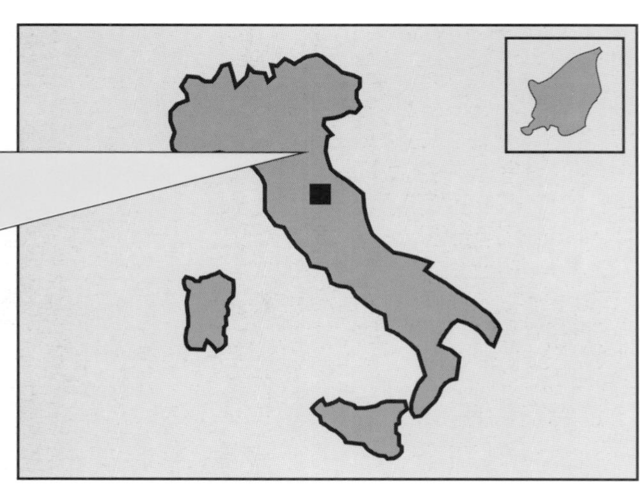

Starting grid

Row	Driver	Team	Time	Speed
1	J. Villeneuve	Williams	1'23"303	(213,054)
1	H. H. Frentzen	Williams	1'23"646	(212,180)
2	M. Schumacher	Ferrari	1'23"955	(211,399)
2	O. Panis	Prost	1'24"075	(211,097)
3	R. Schumacher	Jordan	1'24"081	(211,082)
3	G. Fisichella	Jordan	1'24"596	(209,797)
4	J. Herbert	Sauber	1'24"723	(209,483)
4	M. Hakkinen	McLaren	1'24"812	(209,263)
5	E. Irvine	Ferrari	1'24"861	(209,142)
5	D. Coulthard	McLaren	1'25"077	(208,611)
6	G. Berger	Benetton	1'25"371	(207,893)
6	N. Larini	Sauber	1'25"544	(207,472)
7	R. Barrichello	Stewart	1'25"579	(207,387)
7	J. Alesi	Benetton	1'25"729	(207,024)
8	D. Hill	Arrows	1'25"743	(206,991)
8	J. Magnussen	Stewart	1'26"192	(205,912)
9	P. Diniz	Arrows	1'26"253	(205,767)
9	S. Nakano	Prost	1'26"712	(204,678)
10	M. Salo	Tyrrell	1'26"852	(204,348)
10	J. Trulli	Minardi	1'26"960	(204,094)
11	J. Verstappen	Tyrrell	1'27"428	(203,001)
11	U. Katayama	Minardi	1'28"727	(200,029)

Imola is less than 80 kilometres from Maranello, so it is logical that Ferrari feels at home. But this, together with the fact that the circuit is dedicated to Enzo and Dino Ferrari, did not explain why the red cars returned to form in the race after being outqualified by the Williams in qualifying.
The British car won again, making it three victories in the last three races.
But this time Villeneuve had gearbox problems two-thirds into the race, together with a tactical miscomprehension with the team.
The top podium slot went to Frentzen for the first time, but despite this result, the Williams team was far from happy.
Frentzen just made it to the line ahead of a Ferrari, as in Argentina. This time Schumacher - now second in the championship - did not have to thank the physical condition of the winner for his runner-up slot.
This time the Ferrari was right on the pace. His race fastest lap was just 6/1000ths of a second slower than the winner's.
As if that was not enough, third went to Irvine in another display of Ferrari reliability. The rest at Imola were nowhere to be seen.
Fourth was Giancarlo Fisichella, who scored his first points of the season and who was becoming more and more impressive race after race.
Fifth was Alesi, ahead of Hakkinen, who scored points for the fourth time in four GPs and who was now third equal in the championship with Coulthard, Berger and Frentzen.
Imola went down into the record-books with another strong performance from the Williams but the Ferrari F310B seemed to be on the right track ... towards victory.

Results

	Driver	Car	Avg.	Gap
1	H.H. Frentzen	Williams	201.509	
2	M. Schumacher	Ferrari	201.464	1"237
3	E. Irvine	Ferrari	198.659	1'18"343
4	G. Fisichella	Jordan	198.478	1'23"388
5	J. Alesi	Benetton	197.630	1 lap
6	M. Hakkinen	McLaren	197.613	1 lap
7	N. Larini	Sauber	196.863	1 lap
8	O. Panis	Prost	196.244	1 lap
9	M. Salo	Tyrrell	194.850	2 laps
10	J. Verstappen	Tyrrell	194.614	2 laps
11	U. Katayama	Minardi	189.907	3 laps

Retirements

Driver	Car	Lap	Raison
J. Trulli	Minardi	0	Gear
J. Magnussen	Stewart	2	Spunn off
G. Berger	Benetton	4	Spunn off
D. Hill	Arrows	11	Accident
S. Nakano	Prost	11	Accident
R. Schumacher	Jordan	17	Axle-shaft
J. Herbert	Sauber	18	Electrical fault
R. Barrichello	Stewart	32	Oil pressure
D. Coulthard	McLaren	38	Engine
J. Villeneuve	Williams	40	Gear
P. Diniz	Arrows	53	Gear

Topspeed

Driver	Max.
Villeneuve	286.400
Fisichella	286.400
Frentzen	284.900
Irvine	284.900
R. Schumacher	284.200
Hakkinen	284.200
M. Schumacher	284.200
Coulthard	283.400
Nakano	283.400
Panis	282.700
Berger	282.700
Herbert	281.900
Larini	281.200
Alesi	280.500
Barrichello	279.700
Hill	279.700
Magnussen	279.000

Another Williams' triumph at Imola ... this time not with Villeneuve. The ten points went to H.H. Frentzen, who scored the first win of his 52-race F1 career, becoming the fourth German driver to win a Grand Prix, after Wolfgang von Trips (1 win), Jochen Mass (1) and Michael Schumacher (22 so far).
Ninth place for Mika Salo, for whom rumours abound regarding a Ferrari place in 1998.
100th GP for Johnny Herbert, who celebrates with a cake. But in the race, he retired with electrical problems in his Sauber-Ferrari.
The 1997 San Marino GP was the fourth anniversary of the death of Ayrton Senna, to whom a statue was dedicated at the Tamburello curve where the Brazilian driver lost his life on 1st May 1994.

MONACO GP

1990 A. Senna
1991 A. Senna
1992 A. Senna
1993 A. Senna
1994 M. Schumacher
1995 M. Schumacher
1996 O. Panis

THE CIRCUIT

11th May 1997

Circuit: Monaco - **Distance:** Km 208 - **Spectators:** 105.000

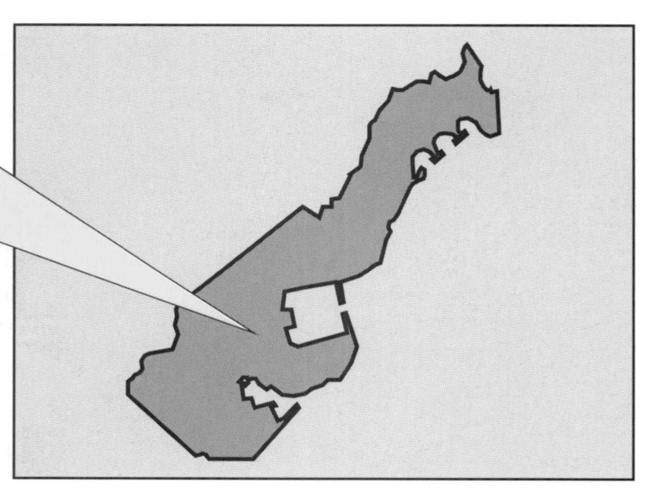

STARTING GRID

Row	Driver	Team	Time	Speed
1	H. H. Frentzen	Williams	1'18"216	(154,971)
1	M. Schumacher	Ferrari	1'18"235	(154,933)
2	J. Villeneuve	Williams	1'18"583	(154,247)
2	G. Fisichella	Jordan	1'18"665	(154,086)
3	D. Coulthard	McLaren	1'18"779	(153,863)
3	R. Schumacher	Jordan	1'18"943	(153,544)
4	J. Herbert	Sauber	1'19"105	(153,229)
4	M. Hakkinen	McLaren	1'19"119	(153,202)
5	J. Alesi	Benetton	1'19"263	(152,924)
5	R. Barrichello	Stewart	1'19"295	(152,862)
6	N. Larini	Sauber	1'19"468	(152,529)
6	O. Panis	Prost	1'19"626	(152,227)
7	D. Hill	Arrows	1'19"674	(152,135)
7	M. Salo	Tyrrell	1'19"694	(152,097)
8	E. Irvine	Ferrari	1'19"723	(152,041)
8	P. Diniz	Arrows	1'19"860	(151,781)
9	G. Berger	Benetton	1'20"199	(151,139)
9	J. Trulli	Minardi	1'20"349	(150,857)
10	J. Magnussen	Stewart	1'20"516	(150,544)
10	U. Katayama	Minardi	1'20"606	(150,376)
11	S. Nakano	Prost	1'20"961	(149,717)
11	J. Verstappen	Tyrrell	1'21"290	(149,111)

The rain came down at Montecarlo and upset the balance in Formula 1. It began to rain just a few minutes before the start of the race ... and panic ensued. Which tyres should be used? What set-up should be chosen? Here Williams committed its first major error of the season.
It had its own personal weather forecast and thought that the storm would not last very long.
The result was that Frentzen and Villeneuve, first and third on the grid, fitted slick, treadless tyres, taking no account of the fact that the rain was falling heavily.
Within the Ferrari team, Schumacher-logic prevailed.
The German opted for intermediates: if it suddenly stopped raining, he would have a few more laps than the opposition to go faster; if it continued raining, his exceptional wet-weather ability would do the rest.
Destiny then took over. As was to be expected, the two Williams slithered away from the grid.
Schumacher took the lead ahead of a splendid Fisichella, who powered away from row 2 with his Jordan.
There were spins and incidents at almost every curve of the street circuit and at the end of the race, 12 of the 22 starters had retired, including the Arrows of Diniz and Hill, the McLarens of Coulthard and Hakkinen and the two Williams of Villeneuve and Frentzen.
Up ahead Schumacher was navigating through the rainy gloom.
He was making no mistakes and going well, building up a lead which ten laps from the end allowed him to rectify a major slide at the St. Devote curve immediately after the pits.
Barrichello finished second behind Schumacher. This was the best result yet for the Stewart team in its first year of F1. Irvine was third, confirming Ferrari's current run of form in the championship.
Schumacher and the Maranello constructor were now both leading their respective standings ... for the first time since the 1990 British GP!

RESULTS

	DRIVER	CAR	AVG.	GAP
1	M. Schumacher	Ferrari	104.295	
2	R. Barrichello	Stewart	103.529	53"306
3	E. Irvine	Ferrari	103.120	1'22"108
4	O. Panis	Prost	102.806	1'44"402
5	M. Salo	Tyrrell	102.434	1 lap
6	G. Fisichella	Jordan	102.335	1 lap
7	J. Magnussen	Stewart	101.113	1 lap
8	J. Verstappen	Tyrrell	100.727	2 laps
9	G. Berger	Benetton	100.394	2 laps
10	U. Katayama	Minardi	99.495	2 laps

RETIREMENTS

DRIVER	CAR	LAP	REASON
P. Diniz	Arrows	0	Accident
D. Hill	Arrows	1	Accident
M. Hakkinen	McLaren	1	Accident
D. Coulthard	McLaren	1	Spunn off
J. Trulli	Minardi	7	Accident
J. Herbert	Sauber	9	Accident
R. Schumacher	Jordan	10	Spunn off
J. Villeneuve	Williams	16	Accident
J. Alesi	Benetton	16	Spunn off
N. Larini	Sauber	24	Spunn off
S. Nakano	Prost	36	Spunn off
H.H. Frentzen	Williams	39	Accident

TOPSPEED

DRIVER	MAX.
Nakano	281.900
Villeneuve	278.300
Frentzen	278.300
Alesi	276.900
Hakkinen	276.200
M. Schumacher	274.800
Panis	274.100
Berger	273.400
Coulthard	272.700
Barrichello	272.700
Irvine	272.000
Fisichella	271.300
R. Schumacher	271.300
Magnussen	271.300
Herbert	269.300
Diniz	269.300
Larini	268.600

First victory of 1997 for Michael Schumacher, who powered his Ferrari to a memorable triumph in a Grand Prix which began in a downpour. Together with him on the podium, Rubens Barrichello and Eddie Irvine, second and third. Ferrari could not have found a better way to celebrate the 50th anniversary of the first-ever participation in a race (the Piacenza GP in 1947) of a Ferrari team.
For Schumacher, victory at Montecarlo (his 23rd in 89 F1 races) put him into the lead of the Drivers' championship, with Ferrari now in command of the Manufacturers' standings.
Barrichello, second at the chequered flag and receiving congratulations from the three-times world champion (1969, '71 and '73) Jackie Stewart, takes the first points for the brand-new Stewart team.
Only sixth Giancarlo Fisichella, who had come close to pole position in qualifying with the Jordan-Peugeot.

Spanish GP

1990 A. Prost
1991 N. Mansell
1992 N. Mansell
1993 A. Prost
1994 D. Hill
1995 M. Schumacher
1996 M. Schumacher

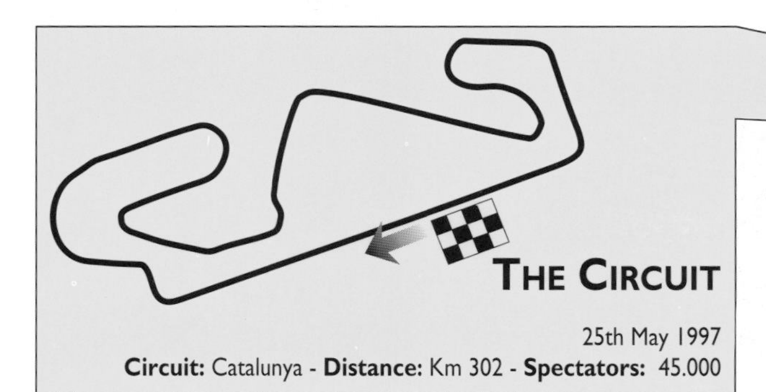

The Circuit

25th May 1997

Circuit: Catalunya - **Distance:** Km 302 - **Spectators:** 45.000

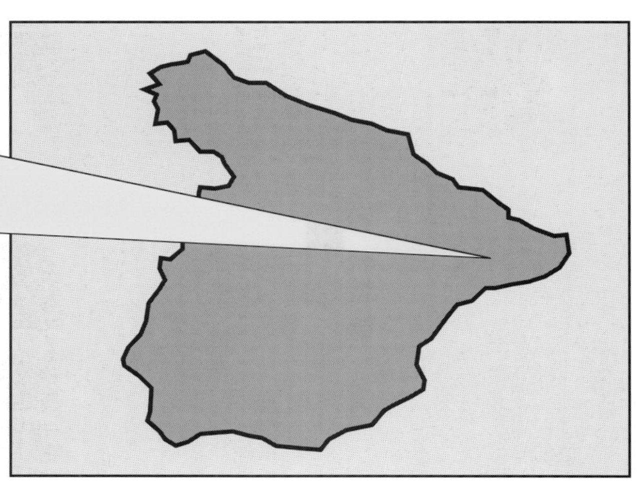

Starting grid

Pos.	Driver	Team	Time	Speed
1	J. Villeneuve	Williams	1'16"525	(222,421)
	H. H. Frentzen	Williams	1'16"791	(221,651)
2	D. Coulthard	McLaren	1'17"521	(219,564)
	J. Alesi	Benetton	1'17"717	(219,010)
3	M. Hakkinen	McLaren	1'17"737	(218,954)
	G. Berger	Benetton	1'18"041	(218,101)
4	M. Schumacher	Ferrari	1'18"313	(217,343)
	G. Fisichella	Jordan	1'18"385	(217,144)
5	R. Schumacher	Jordan	1'18"423	(217,038)
	J. Herbert	Sauber	1'18"494	(216,842)
6	E. Irvine	Ferrari	1'18"873	(215,800)
	O. Panis	Prost	1'19"157	(215,026)
7	G. Morbidelli	Sauber	1'19"323	(214,576)
	M. Salo	Tyrrell	1'20"079	(212,550)
8	D. Hill	Arrows	1'20"089	(212,524)
	S. Nakano	Prost	1'20"103	(212,486)
9	R. Barrichello	Stewart	1'20"255	(212,084)
	J. Trulli	Minardi	1'20"452	(211,565)
10	J. Verstappen	Tyrrell	1'20"582	(211,223)
	U. Katayama	Minardi	1'20"672	(210,988)
11	P. Diniz	Arrows	1'21"029	(210,058)
	J. Magnussen	Stewart	1'21"060	(209,978)

The Spanish GP is traditionally favourable to Williams, which has always best been able to interpret the difficult characteristics of the Montmelò circuit north of Barcellona.
This year Jacques Villeneuve added something else to the tradition: together with his chief engineer Jock Clear, he began to work independently from the rest of the team to obtain an exceptional set-up for his Williams.
In Spain, performance wasn't the only thing that counted: tyre wear was also important.
Jacques hit the mark with his fifth pole of the season (six out of six for Williams) and his third win of the year, which took himself and his team back to the top of the championships.
The Spanish GP was all about Williams' return to dominant form.
The setback at Montecarlo had failed to disturb Villeneuve, who was as brilliant and determined as ever, while Ferrari was back on the defensive.
Seventh on the grid with Schumacher and eleventh with Irvine, the team was hoping to reduce tyre wear to a minimum.
Schumacher finished fourth behind Villeneuve, Panis with the Prost and a brilliant Alesi with the Benetton.
He lost his championship lead but was only three points behind the Canadian.
Ferrari was still ahead in the manufacturers' race, just one point ahead of Williams.
All things considered, it was a positive result for Ferrari.
The Catalan circuit was without a doubt Ferrari's worst circuit in the first half of the season.
Only the rain could have given Schumacher a chance (remember his win in 1996!), but after a few drops on Sunday morning, the race was held entirely in the dry.

Results

	Driver	Car	Avg.	Gap
1	J. Villeneuve	Williams	200.396	
2	O. Panis	Prost	200.182	5"804
3	J. Alesi	Benetton	199.935	12"534
4	M. Schumacher	Ferrari	199.735	17"979
5	J. Herbert	Sauber	199.369	27"986
6	D. Coulthard	McLaren	199.305	29"744
7	M. Hakkinen	McLaren	198.613	48"785
8	H.H. Frentzen	Williams	198.059	1'04"139
9	G. Fisichella	Jordan	198.036	1'04"767
10	G. Berger	Benetton	198.004	1'05"670
11	J. Verstappen	Tyrrell	196.269	1 lap
12	E. Irvine	Ferrari	195.488	1 lap
13	J. Magnussen	Stewart	194.304	1 lap
14	G. Morbidelli	Sauber	193.628	2 laps
15	J. Trulli	Minardi	193.299	2 laps

Retirements

Driver	Car	Lap	Reason
U. Katayama	Minardi	11	Gear
D. Hill	Arrows	18	Engine
S. Nakano	Prost	34	Gear
M. Salo	Tyrrell	35	Tyre sx.
R. Barrichello	Stewart	37	Engine
R. Schumacher	Jordan	50	Engine
P. Diniz	Arrows	53	Engine

Topspeed

Driver	Max.
Villeneuve	293.400
Alesi	291.100
Herbert	290.300
Hakkinen	290.300
Fisichella	289.500
Coulthard	289.500
Frentzen	288.700
Morbidelli	288.700
R. Schumacher	288.000
Nakano	287.200
Berger	287.200
Panis	286.400
M. Schumacher	286.400
Magnussen	285.700
Irvine	285.700
Barrichello	284.900
Verstappen	281.900

Third win of 1997 in six races (in the other three he retired) for Jacques Villeneuve, spraying the champagne on the podium together with Jean Alesi, who was third for Benetton. The Grand Prix was conditioned by the tyre factor and many teams had enormous problems lasting the race, with massive blisters appearing on the tyre tread.
John Barnard, former Ferrari, McLaren and Benetton designer, reappeared in Spain in the Arrows team, replacing Frank Dernie as technical director.
Verstappen, eleventh at the finish, here seen with his Tyrrell ahead of Diniz (Arrows), who retired from the race together with his teammate Hill.

Canadian GP

1990 A. Senna
1991 N. Piquet
1992 G. Berger
1993 A. Prost
1994 M. Schumacher
1995 J. Alesi
1996 D. Hill

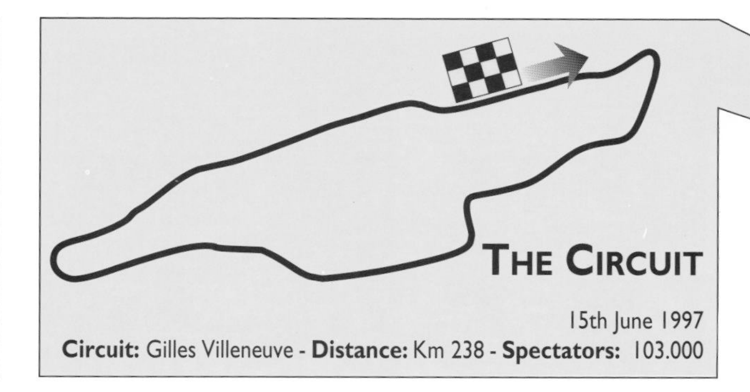

The Circuit

15th June 1997
Circuit: Gilles Villeneuve - **Distance:** Km 238 - **Spectators:** 103.000

Starting grid

Row		
1	M. Schumacher Ferrari 1'18"095 (203,798)	J. Villeneuve Williams 1'18"108 (203,764)
2	R. Barrichello Stewart 1'18"388 (203,036)	H. H. Frentzen Williams 1'18"464 (202,840)
3	D. Coulthard McLaren 1'18"466 (202,834)	G. Fisichella Jordan 1'18"750 (202,103)
4	R. Schumacher Jordan 1'18"869 (201,798)	J. Alesi Benetton 1'18"899 (201,721)
5	M. Hakkinen McLaren 1'18"916 (201,678)	O. Panis Prost 1'19"034 (201,377)
6	A. Wurz Benetton 1'19"286 (200,737)	E. Irvine Ferrari 1'19"503 (200,189)
7	J. Herbert Sauber 1'19"622 (199,889)	J. Verstappen Tyrrell 1'20"102 (198,692)
8	D. Hill Arrows 1'20"129 (198,625)	P. Diniz Arrows 1'20"175 (198,511)
9	M. Salo Tyrrell 1'20"336 (198,113)	G. Morbidelli Sauber 1'20"357 (198,061)
10	S. Nakano Prost 1'20"370 (198,029)	J. Trulli Minardi 1'20"370 (198,029)
11	J. Magnussen Stewart 1'20"491 (197,731)	U. Katayama Minardi 1'21"034 (196,406)

A revolution was about to take place in Formula 1. Without the aid of the rain, Michael Schumacher and Ferrari dominated the seventh round of the world championship. The German obtained the first non-Williams pole of the year with a superb lap that relegated local hero Villeneuve to second place on the grid by just 13/1000ths of a second.
He then went on to take his second win of the year: his best so far, even though it came with a little help from Villeneuve.
Jacques was clearly the home favourite at Montreal. But when he arrived, his nerves were a little shaky. He had just jetted back from a flight over the ocean to Paris, where the International Federation had summoned him to explain his 'careless' declarations over the new 1998 regulations.
But maybe this was all just a smokescreen, because the Canadian was almost on pole and Ferrari would probably have suffered tyre problems in the race.
Yet Jacques managed to commit an incredible error.
At the end of lap 2, when he was right on leader Schumacher's exhausts, he made a mistake at the chicane before the pits and ended up against the wall.
Too much tension? Maybe.
The fact is that Michael won (thanks also to a mechanical problem on the McLaren of Coulthard who had made the right tyre choice) and moved back into the lead of the championship by seven points.
Ferrari was now also eight points ahead in the manufacturers' race.
One final comment: the tyre war between Goodyear and Bridgestone was hotting up.
The first to come off worse from this battle was probably Olivier Panis, who crashed his Prost against the barriers three laps from the end and broke both his legs.
He would be out for at least four months.

Results

	Driver	Car	Avg.	Gap
1	M. Schumacher	Ferrari	184.404	
2	J. Alesi	Benetton	184.303	2"565
3	G. Fisichella	Jordan	184.277	3"219
4	H.H. Frentzen	Williams	184.255	3"768
5	J. Herbert	Sauber	184.218	4"716
6	S. Nakano	Prost	182.963	36"701
7	D. Coulthard	McLaren	182.922	37"753
8	P. Diniz	Arrows	180.968	1 lap
9	D. Hill	Arrows	180.914	1 lap
10	G. Morbidelli	Sauber	180.778	1 lap
11	O. Panis	Prost	184.174	3 laps

Retirements

Driver	Car	Lap	Reason
M. Hakkinen	McLaren	0	Accident
E. Irvine	Ferrari	0	Accident
J. Magnussen	Stewart	0	Accident
J. Villeneuve	Williams	1	Accident
U. Katayama	Minardi	5	Accident
R. Schumacher	Jordan	14	Accident
J. Trulli	Minardi	32	Engine
R. Barrichello	Stewart	33	Gear
A. Wurz	Benetton	35	Transmission
J. Verstappen	Tyrrell	42	Gear
M. Salo	Tyrrell	46	Engine

Topspeed

Driver	Max.
Wurz	295.000
Villeneuve	293.400
M. Schumacher	293.400
R. Schumacher	292.600
Frentzen	291.800
Irvine	291.800
Hakkinen	291.800
Fisichella	291.800
Alesi	291.100
Barrichello	290.300
Panis	289.500
Herbert	289.500
Coulthard	288.700
Nakano	288.000
Salo	287.200
Diniz	286.400
Morbidelli	286.400

Second win of the year for Schumacher and Ferrari, who lengthened their lead of the two standings by 7 and 8 points respectively over Villeneuve and Williams. But at Montreal, the spotlights were also on Giancarlo Fisichella: 24 years old from Rome, Fisichella finished third in his Jordan-Peugeot behind Alesi, scoring his first podium finish in his 15-race F1 career. A serious accident however for Olivier Panis who, three laps before the end, had a violent crash in his Prost-Mugen, breaking both legs. His recovery was to last more than three months.

French GP

1990 A. Prost
1991 N. Mansell
1992 N. Mansell
1993 A. Prost
1994 M. Schumacher
1995 M. Schumacher
1996 D. Hill

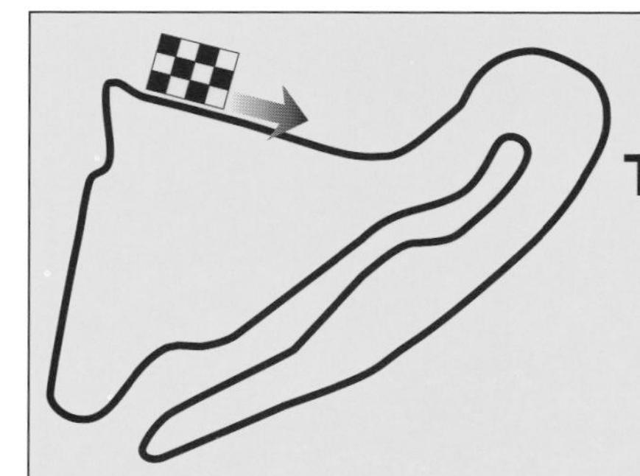

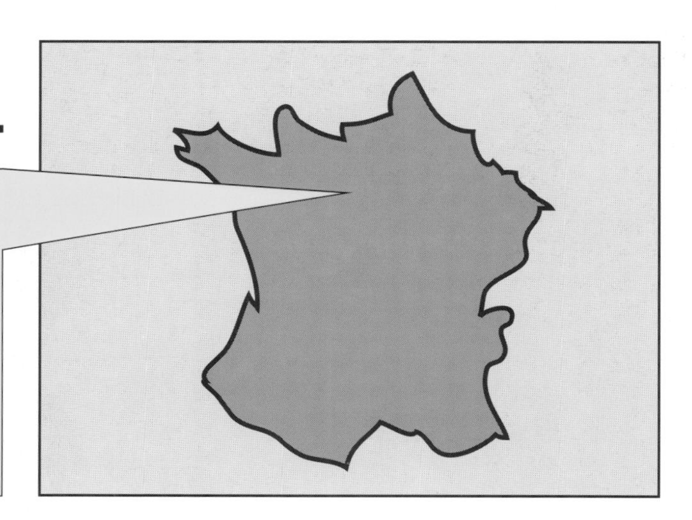

The Circuit

29th June 1997
Circuit: Magny-Cours
Distance: Km 306
Spectators: 100.000

Starting grid

Pos	Driver	Team	Time	Speed
1	M. Schumacher	Ferrari	1'14"548	(205,237)
1	H. H. Frentzen	Williams	1'14"749	(204,685)
2	R. Schumacher	Jordan	1'14"755	(204,669)
2	J. Villeneuve	Williams	1'14"800	(204,545)
3	E. Irvine	Ferrari	1'14"860	(204,382)
3	J. Trulli	Prost	1'14"957	(204,117)
4	A. Wurz	Benetton	1'14"986	(204,038)
4	J. Alesi	Benetton	1'15"228	(203,382)
5	D. Coulthard	McLaren	1'15"270	(203,268)
5	M. Hakkinen	McLaren	1'15"339	(203,082)
6	G. Fisichella	Jordan	1'15"453	(202,775)
6	S. Nakano	Prost	1'15"857	(201,695)
7	R. Barrichello	Stewart	1'15"876	(201,645)
7	J. Herbert	Sauber	1'16"018	(201,268)
8	J. Magnussen	Stewart	1'16"149	(200,922)
8	P. Diniz	Arrows	1'16"536	(199,906)
9	D. Hill	Arrows	1'16"729	(199,403)
9	J. Verstappen	Tyrrell	1'16"941	(198,854)
10	M. Salo	Tyrrell	1'17"256	(198,043)
10	N. Fontana	Sauber	1'17"538	(197,323)
11	U. Katayama	Minardi	1'17"563	(197,259)
11	T. Marques	Minardi	1'18"280	(195,452)

The 1997 French GP had only one winner and that was Michael Schumacher. "Magny-Cours is not our track - said the German before the race - We will try and limit the damage". It just wasn't true. Ferrari's and Schumacher's prudence was obvious but at Magny-Cours the F310B worked well.
Pole position, fastest lap and victory. Not just any old victory, Schumacher came home in triumph against all the odds. He dominated qualifying with a car that was almost perfect. Then when thick black clouds appeared overhead just before the start, the circus was resigned to yet another Ferrari victory in the rain. Instead it only began to rain half-way through the race.
At that point, Schumacher had a lead of more than twenty seconds on Frentzen, who had started alongside his fellow-countryman from the front row of the grid.
Nobody - not even in the Williams team - believed that Ferrari could finish the race with only two pit-stops; but when it began to rain it was clear that this was the Prancing Horse's race strategy.
As soon as the circuit was wet, Schumacher slipped into rain mode and left the rest floundering ... on his dry-weather tyres.
At the chequered flag, his margin of victory over Frentzen was more than 23 seconds. Irvine was third, well over one minute down, ahead of Villeneuve who was fourth despite a trip into the grass a few curves from the end. Alesi was fifth after colliding with Coulthard, whose McLaren remained off the track and who would be classified seventh one lap behind, preceeded by Ralf Schumacher in the Jordan.
For Schumacher and Ferrari, the weekend in France was full of satisfaction. The F310B, the creation of John Barnard which was judged to be unsuccessful far too early, had matured and improved. Now it performed well on any circuit, as would be seen starting with the next race ...

Results

	Driver	Car	Avg.	Gap
1	M. Schumacher	Ferrari	185.752	
2	H.H. Frentzen	Williams	185.018	23"537
3	E. Irvine	Ferrari	183.438	1'14"801
4	J. Villeneuve	Williams	183.225	1'21"784
5	J. Alesi	Benetton	183.196	1'22"735
6	R. Schumacher	Jordan	182.979	1'29"871
7	D. Coulthard	McLaren	183.479	1 lap
8	J. Herbert	Sauber	181.781	1 lap
9	G. Fisichella	Jordan	180.561	1 lap
10	J. Trulli	Prost	179.503	2 laps
11	U. Katayama	Minardi	178.441	2 laps
12	D. Hill	Arrows	177.411	3 laps

Retirements

Driver	Car	Lap	Reason
T. Marques	Minardi	5	Engine
S. Nakano	Prost	7	Spunn off
J. Verstappen	Tyrrell	15	Crashed
M. Hakkinen	McLaren	18	Engine
J. Magnussen	Stewart	33	Brakes
R. Barrichello	Stewart	36	Engine
N. Fontana	Sauber	40	Spunn off
P. Diniz	Arrows	58	Crashed
A. Wurz	Benetton	60	Crashed
M. Salo	Tyrrell	61	Electrical fault

Topspeed

Driver	Max.
Fisichella	296.700
R. Schumacher	295.800
Wurz	291.800
Frentzen	291.800
Villeneuve	291.800
Hakkinen	291.100
Alesi	290.300
Trulli	289.500
Coulthard	289.500
Magnussen	288.700
Nakano	288.700
M. Schumacher	288.700
Fontana	287.200
Diniz	286.400
Irvine	285.700
Barrichello	284.900
Herbert	284.900

Three!! Schumacher took his Ferrari to the top podium slot at Magny-Cours and now had 14 points lead in the Drivers' championship. Thanks also to the third place of Irvine - who was beaten only by his teammate and by Frentzen - Ferrari's lead in the championship was increased to 13 points over a crisis-ridden Williams. Villeneuve could only finish fourth after going off the road in the final few curves.
The French GP also saw some fresh new faces. Argentinian Norberto Fontana took the place of an injured Morbidelli in the number 17 Sauber. Jarno Trulli instead focuses his gaze on the Prost-Mugen of the injured Panis.
He would take it to tenth place in the race.

British GP

1990	A. Prost
1991	N. Mansell
1992	N. Mansell
1993	A. Prost
1994	D. Hill
1995	J. Herbert
1996	J. Villeneuve

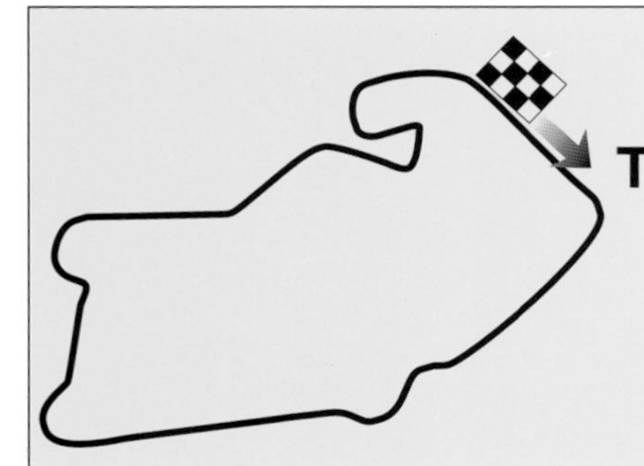

The Circuit

13th July 1997

Circuit: Silverstone

Distance: Km 303

Spectators: 90.000

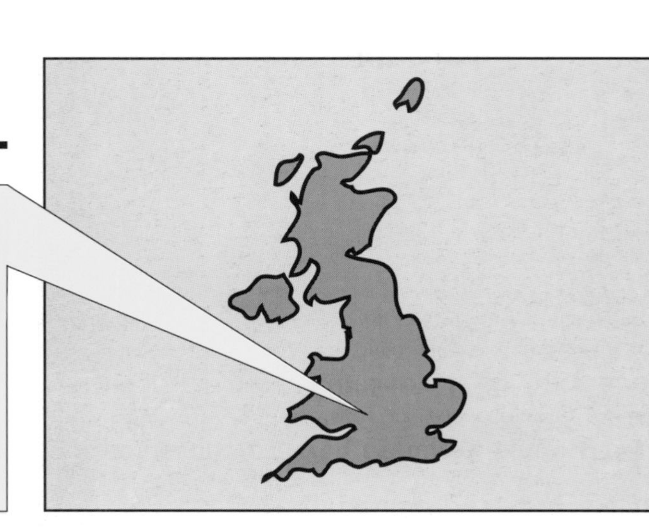

Starting grid

Pos	Driver	Team	Time	Speed
1	J. Villeneuve	Williams	1'21"598	(226,770)
1	H. H. Frentzen	Williams	1'21"732	(226,398)
2	M. Hakkinen	McLaren	1'21"797	(226,219)
2	M. Schumacher	Ferrari	1'21"977	(225,722)
3	R. Schumacher	Jordan	1'22"277	(224,899)
3	D. Coulthard	McLaren	1'22"279	(224,893)
4	E. Irvine	Ferrari	1'22"342	(224,721)
4	A. Wurz	Benetton	1'22"344	(224,716)
5	J. Herbert	Sauber	1'22"368	(224,650)
5	G. Fisichella	Jordan	1'22"371	(224,642)
6	J. Alesi	Benetton	1'22"392	(224,585)
6	D. Hill	Arrows	1'23"271	(222,214)
7	J. Trulli	Prost	1'23"366	(221,961)
7	S. Nakano	Prost	1'23"887	(220,582)
8	J. Magnussen	Stewart	1'24"067	(220,110)
8	P. Diniz	Arrows	1'24"239	(219,661)
9	M. Salo	Tyrrell	1'24"478	(219,039)
9	U. Katayama	Minardi	1'24"553	(218,845)
10	J. Verstappen	Tyrrell	1'25"010	(217,669)
10	T. Marques	Minardi	1'25"154	(217,300)
11	R. Barrichello	Stewart	1'25"525	(216,358)
11	N. Fontana	Sauber	S. T.	

Williams risked a 'knock-out' on their home circuit. Before the Silverstone race, like a fortnight before in France, Ferrari gave itself very few chances of victory. Once again it managed to overturn all expectations: in qualifying Schumacher was fourth, while pole went to Villeneuve ahead of Frentzen and Hakkinen, yet in the race, Schumacher took command and was uncatchable. Almost two-thirds of the way in, Schumacher and Ferrari had victory in the bag. The German was flying on the fast Silverstone curves and the only driver who could keep up with him was Hakkinen. Villeneuve was struggling. Even Silverstone, the heart of British motor racing, was seeing red. Ferrari appeared to be light-years ahead of the home-based Williams team. As Schumacher had 14 points lead over the Canadian before the race, victory for the Ferrari driver would have further increased his chances of taking the world title. But misfortune was lurking around the corner.

Until now, no Ferrari had suffered mechanical failure. The only retirements for the Ferrari F310B had been due to race incidents. This time however, Schumacher's Ferrari suddenly had wheel-bearing failure and the German had to kiss goodbye to victory.

Six laps later, Irvine rolled to a halt after a pit-stop with a broken driveshaft. The world championship situation had changed in just a few curves. Hakkinen's McLaren was leading and with just six laps to go, it seemed as if victory was his. But then the 10 cylinder Mercedes engine began to smoke and the Finn came to a stop just six laps short of his first win, handing Villeneuve his fourth of the season. The Canadian had managed to make up 10 points on Schumacher and was now only 4 behind the German.

Results

	Driver	Car	Avg.	Gap
1	J. Villeneuve	Williams	206.703	
2	J. Alesi	Benetton	206.304	10"205
3	A. Wurz	Benetton	206.262	11"296
4	D. Coulthard	McLaren	205.488	31"229
5	R. Schumacher	Jordan	205.463	31"880
6	D. Hill	Arrows	203.864	1'13"552
7	G. Fisichella	Jordan	203.044	1 lap
8	J. Trulli	Prost	202.695	1 lap
9	N. Fontana	Sauber	201.388	1 lap
10	T. Marques	Minardi	199.929	1 lap
11	S. Nakano	Prost	198.882	2 laps

Retirements

Driver	Car	Lap	Reason
U. Katayama	Minardi	0	Accident
H.H. Frentzen	Williams	0	Accident
P. Diniz	Arrows	29	Distribution
R. Barrichello	Stewart	37	Engine
M. Schumacher	Ferrari	38	Bearing wheel
J. Herbert	Sauber	42	Electrical fault
M. Salo	Tyrrell	44	Engine
E. Irvine	Ferrari	44	Axle-shaft
J. Verstappen	Tyrrell	45	Engine
J. Magnussen	Stewart	50	Engine
M. Hakkinen	McLaren	52	Engine

Topspeed

Driver	Max.
Fisichella	302.500
R. Schumacher	301.600
Villeneuve	300.000
Hakkinen	300.000
Herbert	299.100
Coulthard	299.100
Wurz	298.300
Frentzen	298.300
Alesi	298.300
Magnussen	298.300
M. Schumacher	297.500
Trulli	296.700
Nakano	296.700
Fontana	296.700
Irvine	295.000
Salo	290.300
Hill	290.300

It's not enough to have the number 1 on your car, nor to sign autographs at your home race. Damon Hill, the reigning world champion, had to settle for 12th place on the grid with his Arrows-Yamaha. Luckily, in the race he managed a sixth place which gave him his first points of the season. Eddie Irvine ... yawning! Ferrari seemed to be heading for a superb victory with Schumacher, and his teammate was also going well. But both Ferraris retired with mechanical problems and the champagne on the podium was opened by Jacques Villeneuve. His fourth win of the year took him to within four points of Schumacher in the standings.

GERMAN GP

1990 A. Senna
1991 N. Mansell
1992 N. Mansell
1993 A. Prost
1994 G. Berger
1995 M. Schumacher
1996 D. Hill

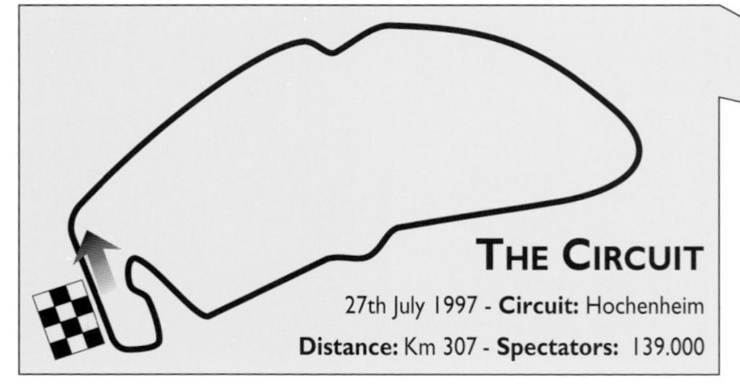

THE CIRCUIT

27th July 1997 - **Circuit:** Hochenheim

Distance: Km 307 - **Spectators:** 139.000

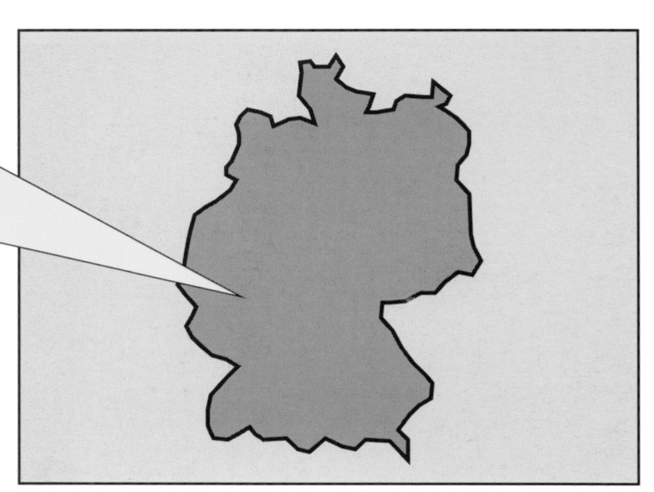

STARTING GRID

1 G. BERGER Benetton 1'41"873 (241,112)	G. FISICHELLA Jordan 1'41"896 (241,058)
2 M. HAKKINEN McLaren 1'42"034 (240,732)	M. SCHUMACHER Ferrari 1'42"181 (240,385)
3 H. H. FRENTZEN Williams 1'42"421 (239,822)	J. ALESI Benetton 1'42"493 (239,653)
4 R. SCHUMACHER Jordan 1'42"498 (239,642)	D. COULTHARD McLaren 1'42"687 (239,201)
5 J. VILLENEUVE Williams 1'42"967 (238,550)	E. IRVINE Ferrari 1'43"209 (237,991)
6 J. TRULLI Prost 1'43"226 (237,952)	R. BARRICHELLO Stewart 1'43"272 (237,846)
7 D. HILL Arrows 1'43"361 (237,641)	J. HERBERT Sauber 1'43"660 (236,955)
8 J. MAGNUSSEN Stewart 1'43"927 (236,347)	P. DINIZ Arrows 1'44"069 (236,024)
9 S. NAKANO Prost 1'44"112 (235,927)	N. FONTANA Sauber 1'44"552 (234,934)
10 M. SALO Tyrrell 1'45"372 (233,106)	J. VERSTAPPEN Tyrrell 1'45"811 (232,138)
11 T. MARQUES Minardi 1'45"942 (231,851)	U. KATAYAMA Sauber 1'46"499 (230,639)

Hockenheim had to bow down to Gerhard Berger. Not because of the fact that he was the oldest driver around today in F1 or because he returned to the track after a three-race absence for health reasons. It was merely due to the result he achieved at Hockenheim.
The Austrian driver, 38 years old on 27th August, strapped himself back into his Benetton, set a fantastic pole position and obtained fastest lap and victory at the German circuit.
Several rumours surrounded Berger before his return.
It was said that breathing problems following bronchitis a few months before, had cleared up, but that he would never have returned to Benetton. It was said that Alexander Wurz, who took his place at the Canadian, French and British GPs, after finishing a superb third at Silverstone, was just too fast and that Berger's performances with the Anglo-Italian car were below par. It was also said that he was still suffering from the recent death of his father, who had died in an air crash in Austria while the driver was convalescing.
Instead the Berger who reappeared at Hockenheim was perfectly intact.
He assured everyone that he was in excellent physical condition.
He insisted that he couldn't wait to drive a F1 car again, and he surprised everyone by saying that next year, should he drive an F1 car again, it would not be for Benetton, which he described rather uncomplimentarily as a 'period which has come to an end'. Then he got into his Benetton and suddenly remembered that Hockenheim has always been one of his favourite circuits. The rest is part of history.
Behind Berger's and Benetton's outstanding victory - off the winner's podium since the 1994 German and 1995 Japanese GPs - Schumacher finished second with the Ferrari, while Villeneuve scored no points after a duel with Trulli (Prost) which finished with the Williams off the track.

RESULTS

	DRIVER	CAR	AVG.	GAP
1	G. Berger	Benetton	227.478	
2	M. Schumacher	Ferrari	226.660	17"527
3	M. Hakkinen	McLaren	226.324	24"770
4	J. Trulli	Prost	226.213	27"165
5	R. Schumacher	Jordan	226.082	29"995
6	J. Alesi	Benetton	225.864	34"717
7	S. Nakano	Prost	223.806	1'19"722
8	D. Hill	Arrows	221.956	1 lap
9	N. Fontana	Sauber	221.520	1 lap
10	J. Verstappen	Tyrrell	219.407	1 lap
11	G. Fisichella	Jordan	224.750	5 laps

RETIREMENTS

DRIVER	CAR	LAP	REASON
E. Irvine	Ferrari	1	Accident
H.H. Frentzen	Williams	1	Accident
D. Coulthard	McLaren	1	Transmission
P. Diniz	Arrows	8	Accident
J. Herbert	Sauber	8	Accident
U. Katayama	Minardi	23	Engine
J. Magnussen	Stewwart	27	Engine
M. Salo	Tyrrell	33	Clutch
R. Barrichello	Stewart	33	Engine
J. Villeneuve	Williams	33	Accident

TOPSPEED

DRIVER	MAX.
Fisichella	349.500
Magnussen	346.100
Fontana	345.000
Herbert	343.900
Hill	343.900
Irvine	343.900
Berger	343.900
Frentzen	343.900
Hakkinen	343.900
Coulthard	342.800
Alesi	342.800
M. Schumacher	341.700
R. Schumacher	341.700
Barrichello	341,700
Trulli	340.600
Villeneuve	339.600
Diniz	338.500

In a certain sense, Hockenheim was ... a veterans' GP. Not just because the 1950s' Silver Arrows Mercedes paraded before the start, as per tradition. But also thanks to the return of Gerhard Berger to F1 after a three-race absence for health reasons. Berger was considered to be an 'ex' of the Circus. Instead he took his rightful place back from Wurz and obtained pole position, fastest lap and race victory, earning himself a champagne shower from Michael Schumacher and Mika Hakkinen, who finished second and third. For Gerhard, 38 years old on 27th August and 203 GPs disputed, this was the tenth victory in F1. Schumacher also had reason to celebrate: with the retirement of Villeneuve, his second place gave him a 10-point lead in the championship.

Hungarian GP

1990 T. Boutsen
1991 A. Senna
1992 A. Senna
1993 D. Hill
1994 M. Schumacher
1995 D. Hill
1996 J. Villeneuve

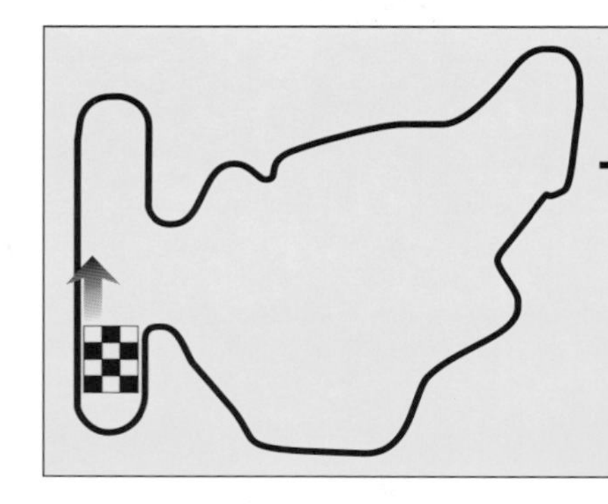

The Circuit

10th August 1997
Circuit: Hungaroring
Distance: Km 305
Spectators: 120.000

Starting grid

Row		
1	**M. Schumacher** Ferrari 1'14"672 (191,301)	**J. Villeneuve** Williams 1'14"859 (190,823)
2	**D. Hill** Arrows 1'15"044 (190,352)	**M. Hakkinen** McLaren 1'15"140 (190,109)
3	**E. Irvine** Ferrari 1'15"424 (189,393)	**H. H. Frentzen** Williams 1'15"520 (189,153)
4	**G. Berger** Benetton 1'15"699 (188,705)	**D. Coulthard** McLaren 1'15"705 (188,690)
5	**J. Alesi** Benetton 1'15"905 (188,199)	**R. Barrichello** Stewart 1'16"138 (187,617)
6	**J. Herbert** Sauber 1'16"138 (187,617)	**J. Trulli** Prost 1'16"297 (187,226)
7	**G. Fisichella** Jordan 1'16"300 (187,219)	**R. Schumacher** Jordan 1'16"686 (186,277)
8	**G. Morbidelli** Sauber 1'16"766 (186,082)	**S. Nakano** Prost 1'16"784 (186,039)
9	**J. Magnussen** Stewart 1'16"858 (185,860)	**J. Verstappen** Tyrrell 1'17"095 (185,288)
10	**P. Diniz** Arrows 1'17"118 (185,233)	**U. Katayama** Minardi 1'17"232 (184,960)
11	**M. Salo** Tyrrell 1'17"482 (184,363)	**T. Marques** Minardi 1'18"020 (183,092)

Sometimes they return ... part two! After Berger's reappearance at Hockenheim, Formula 1 saw another 'resurrection' on the outskirts of Budapest: that of Damon Hill. The return of the 1996 world champion to the 'top' positions was one of the three key topics of the Hungarian GP ... and the most significant. Topic #1 - Hill appeared to be getting rusty during the season due to an Arrows-Yamaha which was far from being the most competitive single-seater in F1. The driver also seemed to have resigned himself to a secondary role. Things changed in Hungary, when the previously slow Arrows suddenly sprouted wings.
His performance was also thanks to the Bridgestone tyres, which were more at home than the Goodyears on the twisty, slippery 4 km Hungaroring track. But this was not sufficient to explain Hill's third fastest time in qualifying. And neither did it explain his performance in the race, which was dominated with class by the British driver after overtaking poleman Schumacher. The dream lasted 75 out of 77 laps, then an electrical fault brought an end to Hill's race and he finished second ... but with a smile on his face.
Topic #2 - Ferrari were supposed to be in difficulty at the Hungaroring. But once the new lightweight chassis (almost 10 kgs less: important because it enabled a better weight distribution for set-up at each circuit) had arrived, Schumacher took pole position. But an 'off' during the warm-up meant that Michael's race car was unusable and that was the only one available. Schumacher started therefore with the 'old' car, which suffered from abnormal tyre wear and which turned his race into a nightmare. Fourth place at the end was almost a gift for the German ... Topic #3 - Villeneuve's luck. The Canadian won without overtaking anybody, thanks to the retirement of the others. For Jacques, it was the fifth victory this year and the second handed to him on a plate after Silverstone. The gap between the Canadian and Schumacher was now 3 points ...

Results

	Driver	Car	Avg.	Gap
1	J. Villeneuve	Williams	173.295	
2	D. Hill	Arrows	173.048	9"079
3	J. Herbert	Sauber	172.739	20"445
4	M. Schumacher	Ferrari	172.466	30"501
5	R. Schumacher	Jordan	172. 460	30"715
6	S. Nakano	Prost	172.169	41"512
7	J. Trulli	Prost	171.257	1'15"552
8	G. Berger	Benetton	171.234	1'16"409
9	E. Irvine	Ferrari	171.048	1 lap
10	U. Katayama	Minardi	171.001	1 lap
11	J. Alesi	Benetton	170.792	1 lap
12	T. Marques	Minardi	167.926	2 laps
13	M. Salo	Tyrrell	167.905	2 laps

Retirements

Driver	Car	Lap	Reason
J. Magnussen	Stewart	5	Steering
G. Morbidelli	Sauber	7	Engine
M. Hakkinen	McLaren	12	Hydraulic circuit
R. Barrichello	Stewart	29	Engine
H.H. Frentzen	Williams	29	Petrol tank
G. Fisichella	Jordan	42	Spunn off
P. Diniz	Arrows	53	Electrical fault
J. Verstappen	Tyrrell	61	Transmission
D. Coulthard	McLaren	65	Alternator

Topspeed

Driver	Max.
Coulthard	276.900
Villeneuve	276.900
M. Schumacher	275.500
Alesi	275.500
Frentzen	274.800
Hakkinen	274.800
Barrichello	274.800
R. Schumacher	274.800
Fisichella	274.100
Irvine	272.700
Magnussen	272.700
Berger	272.000
Herbert	272.000
Diniz	271.300
Trulli	270.600
Hill	270.000
Morbidelli	270.000

Everyone had cause to celebrate on the Hungaroring podium. Especially the blonde (and bleached!) Jacques Villeneuve who scored his fifth win of the year, his ninth overall in only 27 GPs. This success would not have come however, had it not been for the electronic gearbox problems which deprived Damon Hill and the number 1 Arrows-Yamaha of a well-deserved victory two laps from the chequered flag. Villeneuve closed the gap to Schumacher to just three points. The German was fourth with tyre problems. One point went to Japanese driver Nakano, who was sixth with the number 15 Prost-Mugen, the first time he had ever made the top six in the world championship.

Belgian GP

1990 A. Senna
1991 A. Senna
1992 M. Schumacher
1993 D. Hill
1994 D. Hill
1995 M. Schumacher
1996 M. Schumacher

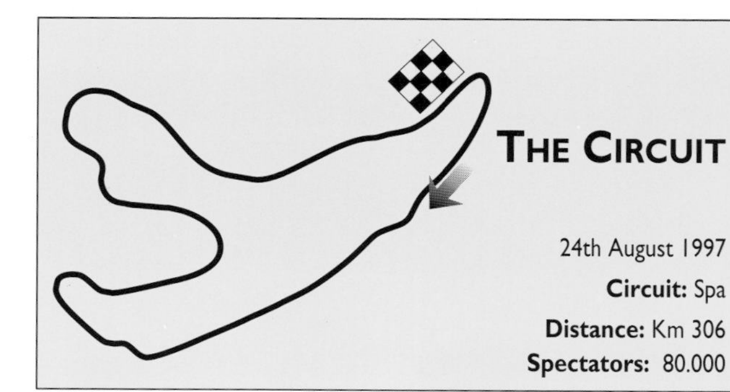

The Circuit

24th August 1997
Circuit: Spa
Distance: Km 306
Spectators: 80.000

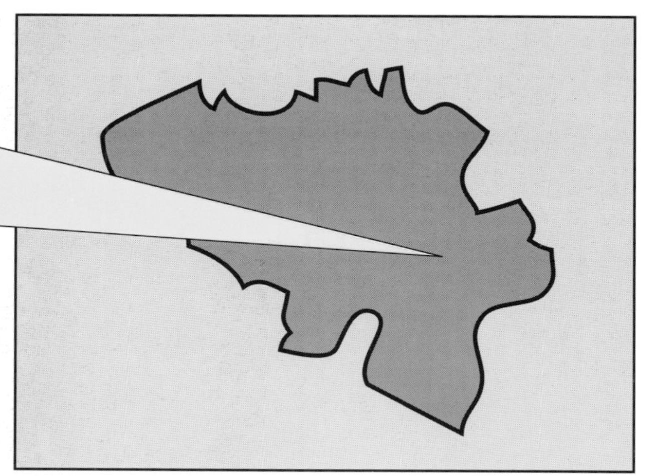

Starting grid

Pos	Driver	Team	Time	Speed
1	J. Villeneuve	Williams	1'49"450	(229,190)
	J. Alesi	Benetton	1'49"759	(228,544)
2	M. Schumacher	Ferrari	1'50"293	(227,438)
	G. Fisichella	Jordan	1'50"470	(227,073)
3	M. Hakkinen	FMcLaren	1'50"503	(227,006)
	R. Schumacher	Jordan	1'50"520	(226,971)
4	H. H. Frentzen	Williams	1'50"656	(226,692)
	P. Diniz	Arrows	1'50"853	(226,289)
5	D. Hill	Arrows	1'50"970	(226,050)
	D. Coulthard	McLaren	1'51"410	(225,158)
6	J. Herbert	Sauber	1'51"725	(224,523)
	R. Barrichello	Stewart	1'51"916	(224,140)
7	G. Morbidelli	Sauber	1'52"094	(223,784)
	J. Trulli	Prost	1'52"274	(223,425)
8	G. Berger	Benetton	1'52"391	(223,192)
	S. Nakano	Prost	1'52"749	(222,484)
9	E. Irvine	Ferrari	1'52"793	(222,397)
	J. Magnussen	Stewart	1'52"886	(222,214)
10	M. Salo	Tyrrell	1'52"897	(222,192)
	U. Katayama	Minardi	1'53"544	(220,926)
11	J. Verstappen	Tyrrell	1'53"725	(220,574)
	T. Marques	Minardi	1'54"505	(219,072)

This Belgian GP will be talked about for years to come: the ability with which Michael Schumacher became the undisputed master of the race on the initial wet surface will form part of motor racing history.
It was a demonstration of sheer driving superiority, one which overcame the limits of technology and which helped the driver become a legend corner after corner.
Twenty minutes to go before the start, a violent storm broke over Spa-Francorchamps.
There was a lot of water on the almost 7 kms Belgian circuit, one of the 'temples' of modern-day F1, and everywhere it was forming puddles, rivulets, damp and flooded areas. The race direction imposed a start behind the safety-car. Schumacher was not aware of this when he decided in any case to start with grooved slicks.
It was very risky: if it began to rain again, he would have had to pit for grooved rain tyres.
Even in these conditions, with intermittent rain on a wet surface, driving on intermediates was crazy. Schumacher accepted the risk: in conditions of virtually non-existent grip, he knew he had an extra gear.
On lap 5, the second after the safety-car had finished its duty, both Alesi and Villeneuve realized this as they were overtaken in the space of six curves in risky moves by the German who powered into the lead. After a few more laps, he had more than 40 seconds lead over his closest rival: that was enough to guarentee the Prancing Horse its fourth win of the season and a considerable points lead in both championships.
Italy had even more cause to celebrate: while Villeneuve could only finish sixth, second place went to the young Giancarlo Fisichella from Rome, the best result of his career.
Things were looking up for the ex-F3 champion.

Results

	Driver	Car	Avg.	Gap
1	M. Schumacher	Ferrari	196.149	
2	G. Fisichella	Jordan	195.221	26"753
3	M. Hakkinen	McLaren	195.079	30"856
4	H.H. Frentzen	Williams	195.035	32"147
5	J. Herbert	Sauber	194.798	39"025
6	J. Villeneuve	Williams	194.692	42"103
7	G. Berger	Benetton	193.952	1'03"741
8	P. Diniz	Arrows	193.198	1'25"931
9	J. Alesi	Benetton	192.656	1'42"008
10	G. Morbidelli	Sauber	192.637	1'42"582
11	E. Irvine	Ferrari	193.024	1 lap
12	M. Salo	Tyrrell	191.663	1 lap
13	J. Magnussen	Stewart	191.281	1 lap
14	D. Hill	Arrows	190.094	2 laps
15	U. Katayama	Minardi	188.462	2 laps
16	J. Trulli	Prost	184.739	2 laps

Retirements

Driver	Car	Lap	Reason
S. Nakano	Prost	5	Electrical
R. Barrichello	Stewart	8	Steering
T. Marques	Minardi	18	Crashed
D. Coulthard	McLaren	19	Spunn off
R. Schumacher	Jordan	21	Spunn off
J. Verstappen	Tyrrell	25	Spunn off

Topspeed

Driver	Max.
Fisichella	318.500
Alesi	316.700
R. Schumacher	316.700
Hill	315.700
Villeneuve	315.700
Diniz	313.900
Frentzen	313.900
Magnussen	313.000
Berger	312.100
Trulli	312.100
Nakano	311.200
Hakkinen	311.200
Coulthard	310.300
Irvine	310.300
Herbert	309.400
Barrichello	309.400
Morbidelli	308.500

Fourth win of the year for Michael Schumacher and Ferrari, who earned a place in the record books in Belgium. On a wet track in the first part of the race, Schumacher set an unassailable pace. In just one lap, he overtook Alesi's Benetton and Villeneuve's Williams and powered away to the flag: it was his 26th F1 win, the 112th for the Prancing Horse, and it took him to a 12-point lead in the championship.
For Williams, Spa was practically a disaster. Frentzen could only finish fourth, Villeneuve sixth and the British team was now 8 points behind Ferrari in the Constructors' battle.

Italian GP

1990 A. Senna
1991 N. Mansell
1992 A. Senna
1993 D. Hill
1994 D. Hill
1995 J. Herbert
1996 M. Schumacher

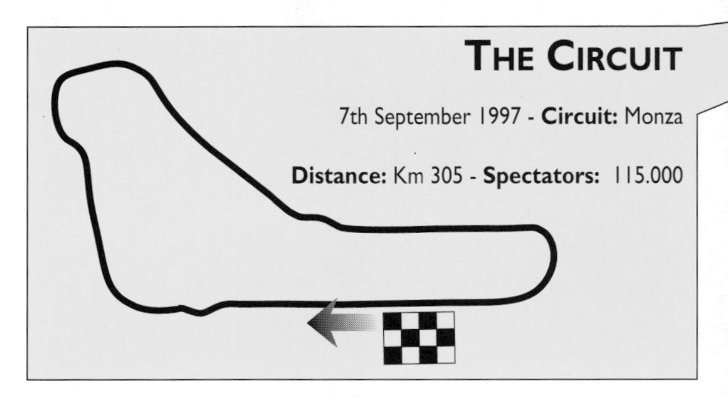

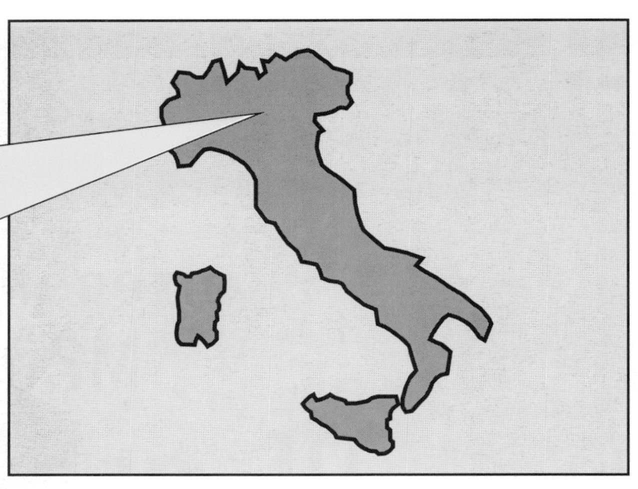

Starting Grid

Row	Driver	Car	Time	Speed
1	J. Alesi	Benetton	1'22"990	(250,295)
1	H. H. Frentzen	Williams	1'23"042	(250,138)
2	G. Fisichella	Jordan	1'23"066	(250,066)
2	J. Villeneuve	Williams	1'23"231	(249,570)
3	M. Hakkinen	McLaren	1'23"340	(249,244)
3	D. Coulthard	McLaren	1'23"347	(249,223)
4	G. Berger	Benetton	1'23"443	(248,936)
4	R. Schumacher	Jordan	1'23"603	(248,460)
5	M. Schumacher	Ferrari	1'23"624	(248,398)
5	E. Irvine	Ferrari	1'23"891	(247,607)
6	R. Barrichello	Stewart	1'24"177	(246,766)
6	J. Herbert	Sauber	1'24"242	(246,575)
7	J. Magnussen	Stewart	1'24"394	(246,131)
7	D. Hill	Arrows	1'24"482	(245,875)
8	S. Nakano	Prost	1'24"553	(245,668)
8	J. Trulli	Prost	1'24"567	(245,628)
9	P. Diniz	Arrows	1'24"639	(245,419)
9	G. Morbidelli	Sauber	1'24"735	(245,141)
10	M. Salo	Tyrrell	1'25"693	(242,400)
10	J. Verstappen	Tyrrell	1'25"845	(241,971)
11	U. Katayama	Minardi	1'26"655	(239,709)
11	T. Marques	Minardi	1'27"677	(236,915)

Ferrari and its driver were now leading both manufacturers' and drivers' standings on the eve of Monza: for the first time since 1979, a year which concluded with Jody Scheckter taking the last title won by a Ferrari driver.
Expectation was fever-pitch over the Italian GP. In the weeks leading up to the race, Monza had been the scene for the official summer test session and more than 15,000 spectators had been present for this pre-race warm-up. The interest of the mass media, both at home and abroad, for the red cars and Schumacher, was growing by the hour. The fans expected Schumacher to win in triumph like the year before.
But things didn't work out that way. At Monza, Ferrari was in all sorts of trouble. During qualifying, both Schumacher and Ferrari were in difficulty: ninth ahead of the other F310B of Irvine. Benetton with Alesi were on pole, followed by the two Williams. Frentzen was second, Villeneuve fourth, split by Fisichella in the Jordan. The third row was all-McLaren with Hakkinen faster than Coulthard. Row 4 was filled by Berger and the other Schumacher, Ralf.
Don't forget the starting-grid order ... because that, at least until the pitstops, was the order in the race. Coulthard and Schumacher (Michael) started well, Villeneuve badly: these were the only changes. The rest of the race was a procession. A high-speed one, but with no overtaking. Alesi lost the lead of the race during the pitstops. Nothing strange here, just that the McLaren mechanics were quicker, sending Coulthard out again in the lead. The only other moment of excitement was a 300 kph collision between Ralf Schumacher and Johnny Herbert in a duel for ninth position. Thankfully it all came to an end with Coulthard's and McLaren's second win of the year. The British driver was followed home by Alesi, Frentzen and Fisichella. The two rivals for the title, Villeneuve and Schumacher, were fifth and sixth. Ferrari and its driver had emerged from Monza virtually unscathed.

Results

	Driver	Car	Avg.	Gap
1	D. Coulthard	McLaren	238.056	
2	J. Alesi	Benetton	237.956	1"937
3	H.H. Frentzen	Williams	237.833	4"343
4	G. Fisichella	Jordan	237.754	5"871
5	J. Villeneuve	Williams	237.726	6"416
6	M. Schumacher	Ferrari	237.466	11"481
7	G. Berger	Benetton	237.416	12"471
8	E. Irvine	Ferrari	237.151	17"639
9	M. Hakkinen	McLaren	235.541	49"373
10	J. Trulli	Prost	234.871	1'02"706
11	S. Nakano	Prost	234.840	1'03"327
12	G. Morbidelli	Sauber	233.044	1 lap
13	R. Barrichello	Stewart	231.014	1 lap
14	T. Marques	Minardi	223.103	3 laps

Retirements

Driver	Car	Lap	Reason
P. Diniz	Arrows	4	Suspension
U. Katayama	Minardi	8	Crashed
J. Verstappen	Tyrrell	12	Gear
J. Magnussen	Stewart	31	Gear
M. Salo	Tyrrell	33	Engine
J. Herbert	Sauber	38	Accident
R. Schumacher	Jordan	39	Suspension
D. Hill	Arrows	46	Engine

Topspeed

Driver	Max.
Coulthard	340.600
Alesi	338.500
Herbert	337.500
Fisichella	336.400
Hakkinen	335.400
Frentzen	334.300
Barrichello	334.300
Morbidelli	334.300
R. Schumacher	333.300
Berger	333.300
Villeneuve	332.300
Irvine	331.200
M. Schumacher	330.200
Diniz	329.200
Magnussenn	329.200
Trulli	327.200
Hill	327.200

Saturday 6th September: an emotional moment at the Italian GP. At noon, all the British teams, mechanics and drivers held a minute's silence in honour of Lady Diana, whose funeral was being broadcast throughout the world at that moment. Then they all concentrated on the race. It was a tough one for Ferrari, who could only manage a sixth place with Schumacher. But Williams couldn't do much better: Frentzen was third, Villeneuve fifth. David Coulthard won his and McLaren's second race of the season and he was followed over the line by Alesi (Benetton), who was leading until the pitstops. Maybe it was also in honour of Jean that the Monza tifosi, partially betrayed by their beloved red cars, spilled onto the track all the same in the classic celebrations beneath the podium.

Austrian GP

1987 N. Mansell

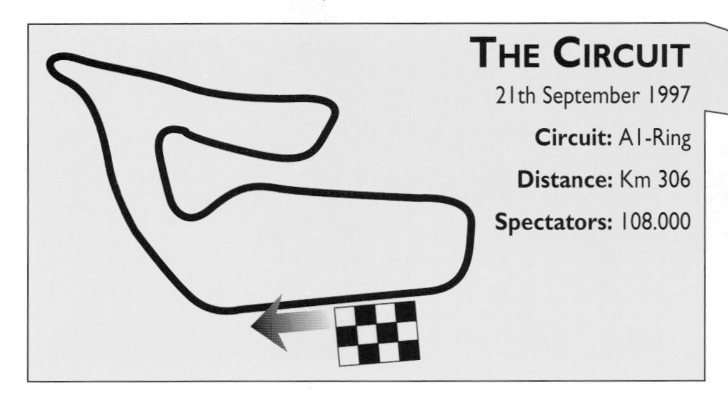

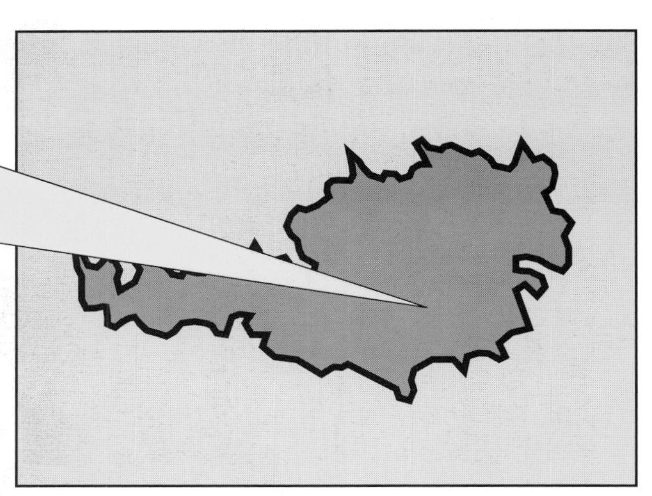

Starting Grid

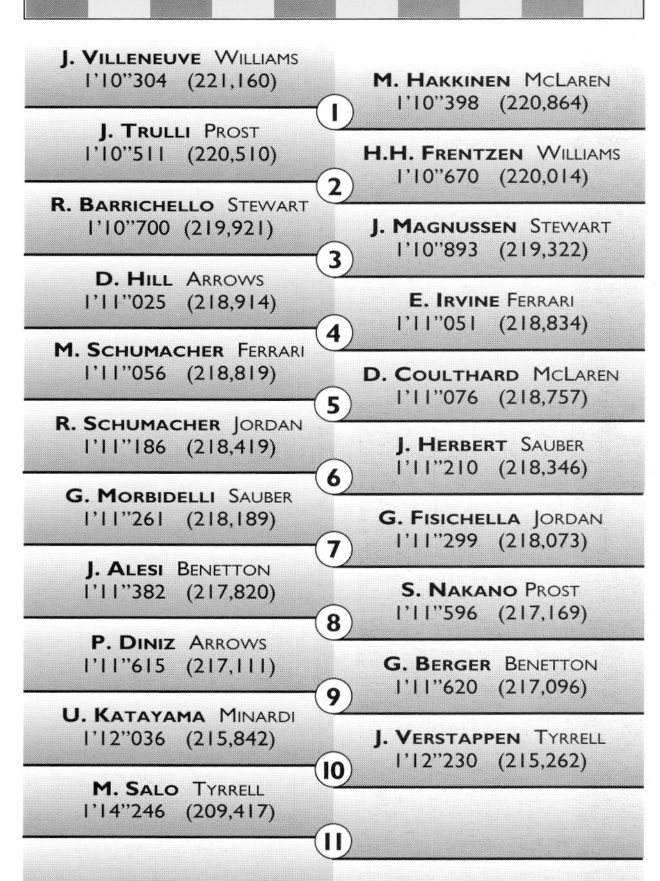

Row		
1	J. Villeneuve Williams 1'10"304 (221,160)	M. Hakkinen McLaren 1'10"398 (220,864)
2	J. Trulli Prost 1'10"511 (220,510)	H.H. Frentzen Williams 1'10"670 (220,014)
3	R. Barrichello Stewart 1'10"700 (219,921)	J. Magnussen Stewart 1'10"893 (219,322)
4	D. Hill Arrows 1'11"025 (218,914)	E. Irvine Ferrari 1'11"051 (218,834)
5	M. Schumacher Ferrari 1'11"056 (218,819)	D. Coulthard McLaren 1'11"076 (218,757)
6	R. Schumacher Jordan 1'11"186 (218,419)	J. Herbert Sauber 1'11"210 (218,346)
7	G. Morbidelli Sauber 1'11"261 (218,189)	G. Fisichella Jordan 1'11"299 (218,073)
8	J. Alesi Benetton 1'11"382 (217,820)	S. Nakano Prost 1'11"596 (217,169)
9	P. Diniz Arrows 1'11"615 (217,111)	G. Berger Benetton 1'11"620 (217,096)
10	U. Katayama Minardi 1'12"036 (215,842)	J. Verstappen Tyrrell 1'12"230 (215,262)
11	M. Salo Tyrrell 1'14"246 (209,417)	

Formula 1 returned to Austria, but the scene this time was nothing like the long curves and the breath-taking rises and descents of the old Osterreichring. The new circuit - which curiously takes its name from the town of Spielberg and not the bordering Zeltweg which characterized the track in the golden days - has no real high-speed points. Not to mention overtaking: almost impossible. A sort of medium-fast circuit, for which Ferrari had ambitious plans. But the practice and qualifying sessions indicated that the situation was not very positive. In his search for a fast time, in fact, Schumacher switched between Friday and Saturday morning from the newly-constructed lighter chassis and the older one. He carried out endless experiments, which ended up by making the engineers lose their way. The result was alarming: the German driver could do no better than ninth on the grid - a disaster. His teammate Irvine was eighth - absurd. Pole position went to Jacques Villeneuve, whose Williams - powered by the latest Renault evolution engine - was back at the front. In contrast to the F310B which seemed to be at the end of its development, the Williams was making progress again. And what progress! The McLarens were outstanding, with Hakkinen on the front row. The Bridgestone-tyred cars were also in superb form: Trulli in the Prost was third, Barrichello (Stewart) was fifth and Hill (Arrows) seventh. On to the Grand Prix. Hakkinen's engine broke down immediately and Trulli incredibly took the lead. He stayed there for half the race, then stopped with engine problems. Villeneuve took over at the front and would stay there until the chequered flag. Schumacher meanwhile was moving up to third place. Then he overtook under yellow flags: the stop-and-go penalty in the pits dropped him outside the points. At the chequered flag, he finished sixth after a superb passing manoeuvre on Hill. Thanks to this point, the German kept the lead in the world championship over the Williams driver.

Results

	Driver	Car	Avg.	Gap
1	J. Villeneuve	Williams	210.228	
2	D. Coulthard	McLaren	210.111	2"909
3	H.H. Frentzen	Williams	210.069	3"962
4	G. Fisichella	Jordan	209.744	12"127
5	R. Schumacher	Jordan	208.961	31"859
6	M. Schumacher	Ferrari	208,900	33"410
7	D. Hill	Arrows	208.750	37"207
8	J. Herbert	Sauber	208.284	49"057
9	G. Morbidelli	Sauber	207.603	1'06"455
10	G. Berger	Benetton	206.840	1 lap
11	U. Katayama	Minardi	203.929	2 laps
12	J. Verstappen	Tyrrell	202.642	2 laps
13	P. Diniz	Arrows	205.968	8 laps
14	R. Barrichello	Stewart	208.444	7 laps

Retirements

Driver	Car	Lap	Reason
M. Hakkinen	McLaren	1	Engine
J. Alesi	Benetton	37	Accident
E. Irvine	Ferrari	38	Accident
M. Salo	Tyrrell	48	Gear
S. Nakano	Prost	57	Engine
J. Magnussen	Stewart	58	Engine
J. Trulli	Prost	58	Engine

Topspeed

Driver	Max.
Magnussen	295.800
Berger	295.000
Morbidelli	294.200
Alesi	293.400
Villeneuve	292.600
Herbert	292.600
Nakano	292.600
Hakkinen	292.600
M. Schumacher	291.800
Barrichello	291.800
Coulthard	291.800
Frentzen	291.100
Trulli	291.100
Irvine	290.300
Fisichella	290.300
Hill	290.300
Diniz	290.300

The first half of the Austrian GP was dominated by Prost and Jarno Trulli. Then the Fench car had mechanical problems, and victory, his sixth of the year, went to Jacques Villeneuve, who won from Coulthard and teammate Frentzen. Eddie Jordan was also happy, but not for the same reason as Villeneuve. In Austria, he presented his new driver for 1998 alongside Ralf Schumacher - the 1996 world champion Damon Hill.

LUXEMBOURG GP

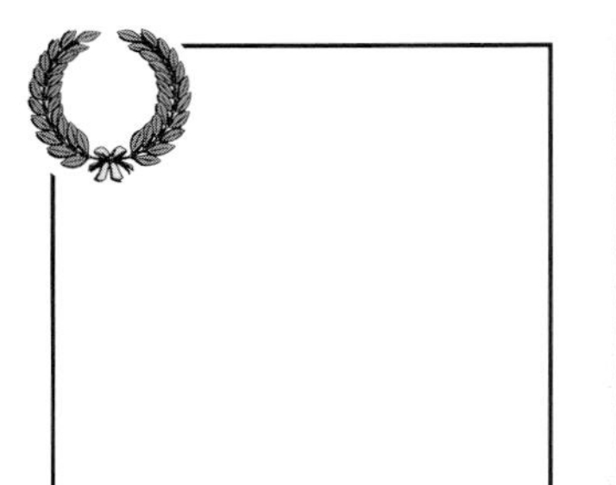

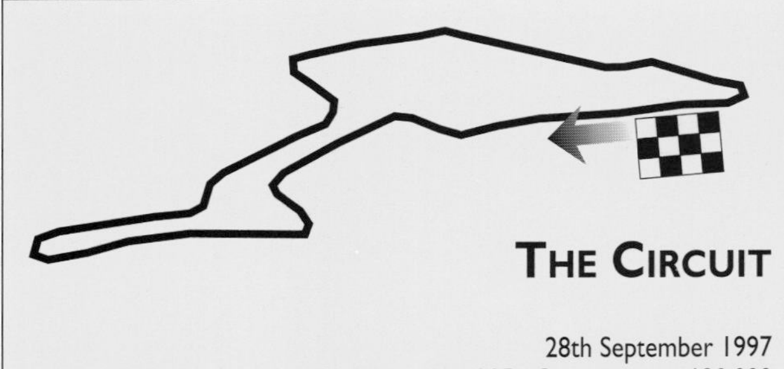

28th September 1997
Circuit: Nürburgring - **Distance:** Km 305 - **Spectators:** 120.000

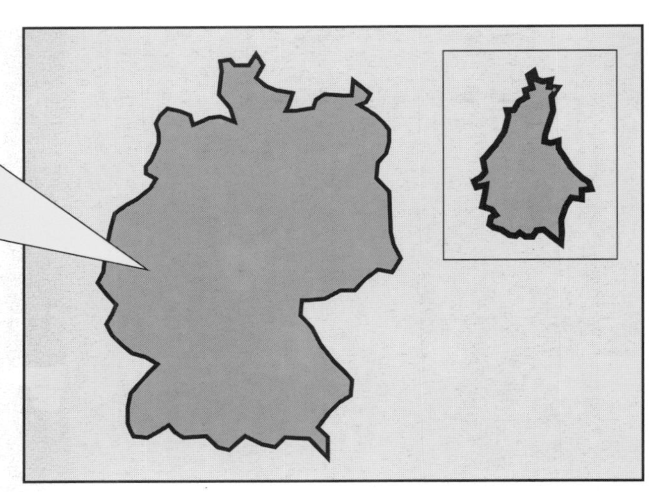

STARTING GRID

Pos	Driver	Time
1	M. HAKKINEN McLAREN	1'16"602 (214,115)
	J. VILLENEUVE WILLIAMS	1'16"691 (213,866)
2	H.H. FRENTZEN WILLIAMS	1'16"741 (213,727)
	G. FISICHELLA JORDAN	1'17"289 (212,211)
3	M. SCHUMACHER FERRARI	1'17"385 (211,948)
	D. COULTHARD McLAREN	1'17"387 (211,943)
4	G. BERGER BENETTON	1'17"587 (211,396)
	R. SCHUMACHER JORDAN	1'17"595 (211,374)
5	R. BARRICHELLO STEWART	1'17"614 (211,323)
	J. ALESI BENETTON	1'17"620 (211,306)
6	O. PANIS PROST	1'17"650 (211,225)
	J. MAGNUSSEN STEWART	1'17"722 (211,029)
7	D. HILL ARROWS	1'17"795 (210,831)
	E. IRVINE FERRARI	1'17"855 (210,669)
8	P. DINIZ ARROWS	1'18"128 (209,932)
	J. HERBERT SAUBER	1'18"303 (209,463)
9	S. NAKANO PROST	1'18"699 (208,409)
	T. MARQUES MINARDI	1'19"347 (206,707)
10	G. MORBIDELLI SAUBER	1'19"490 (206,335)
	M. SALO TYRRELL	1'19"526 (206,242)
11	J. VERSTAPPEN TYRRELL	1'19"531 (206,229)
	U. KATAYAMA MINARDI	1'20"615 (203,456)

Like Spielberg seven days before, the Nürburgring has absolutely nothing in common with the 'impossible to memorize' 23 kilometres of the old Nürburgring, described as the most difficult circuit in motorsport history. On the new circuit, slow and boring, the 1997 world championship played out its third final act. It was a race which was supposed to send Michael Schumacher and his Ferrari well on their way towards the title.
Instead, almost everyone was a protagonist on that four-and-a-half kilometres of track surrounded by a massive crowd which had come to cheer on Schumacher ... except Schumahcer himself.
It would be more correct to say that Schumacher's Ferrari was not a protagonist.
The summer races were now over and the F310B was no longer a victorious car. Meanwhile the Williams and the McLarens had made major progress. Villeneuve looked set for the fastest time, but in the end qualifying saw Mika Hakkinen set the first pole position of his career.
Jacques was second, Schumacher only fifth, but confident in his race set-up. Three curves were all it took to ruin Michael's ambitions and the dreams of the 80,000 spectators. Schumacher started off badly. His brother Ralf on the other hand, got a good start and Michael even had to give way on the right side of the track,
At the first corner the German's Jordan collided with his teammate Fisichella. They were both out, but the worst possible thing happened to Michael, when his brother's car landed on top of him, breaking the front suspension and causing him to retire.
The rest was a bitter pill to swallow for Maranello. The race was dominated by the two McLarens, which both had engine failures, leaving Villeneuve to take the flag.
The Canadian was now leading the Drivers' championship by 9 points from Schumacher, and Williams was now 26 points ahead in the Constructors' standings.

RESULTS

	DRIVER	CAR	AVG.	GAP
1	J. Villeneuve	Williams	200.244	
2	J. Alesi	Benetton	199.815	11"770
3	H.H. Frentzen	Williams	199.753	13"480
4	G. Berger	Benetton	199.647	16"416
5	P. Diniz	Arrows	198.682	43"147
6	O. Panis	Prost	198.660	43"750
7	J. Herbert	Sauber	198.638	44"354
8	D. Hill	Arrows	198.623	44"777
9	G. Morbidelli	Sauber	196.410	1 lap
10	M. Salo	Tyrrell	195.436	1 lap

RETIREMENTS

DRIVER	CAR	LAP	REASON
R. Schumacher	Jordan	0	Starting accident
G. Fisichella	Jordan	0	Starting accident
U. Katayama	Minardi	1	Accident
T. Marques	Minardi	1	Engine
M. Schumacher	Ferrari	2	Suspension
S. Nakano	Prost	16	Engine
E. Irvine	Ferrari	22	Engine
J. Magnussen	Stewart	40	Axle-shaft
D. Coulthard	McLaren	42	Engine
R. Barrichello	Stewart	43	Gear
M. Hakkinen	McLaren	43	Engine
J. Verstappen	Tyrrell	50	Engine

TOPSPEED

DRIVER	MAX.
Coulthard	301.600
Villeneuve	300.000
Hakkinen	299.100
Berger	299.100
M. Schumacher	298.300
R. Schumacher	298.300
Alesi	298.300
Irvine	297.500
Frentzen	297.500
Herbert	297.500
Magnussen	297.500
Fisichella	296.700
Diniz	296.700
Panis	295.800
Barrichello	295.000
Nakano	294.200
Morbidelli	294.200

This year, Nürburgring was all about anniversaries, major changes and celebrations in the pits. At Ferrari, Michael Schumacher celebrated his 100th GP with a cake (in fact, it was his 99th, because he retired before the start of the 1996 French GP). Alongside, from right to left, Ross Brawn, Luca di Montezemolo, Jean Todt, Eddie Irvine and also Bernie Ecclestone, who almost gets the cake in his face. Changing of the guard at Benetton: the final GP for Flavio Briatore, who hands over to David Richards as boss of the team. All-Finnish celebrations for the two Mikas: Hakkinen sets the first pole position of his career; Salo has to settle for a contract signed with Arrows for 1998. And in the grandstands, fans of Schumacher and Villeneuve welcome back Olivier Panis, at the wheel of his Prost again three-and-a-half months after his accident at Montreal.

Autore *Author* *Auteur*	**Roberto Boccafogli**
Fotografia *Photography* Fotografie	**Bryn Williams**
Disegni tecnici *Cutways* Illustrationen *Illustraties*	**Paolo D'Alessio**
Realizzazione grafica *Graphic realization* *Grafische vormgeving*	**Diego Galbiati**
Coordinamento tecnico *Technical coordinator*	**Ermenegildo Chiozzotto**
Traduzioni *Translations* Übersetzung *Vertaling*	**Julian Thomas, Andre' Marzoli, Ivo Op den Camp, Ars Scribendi - Robert Richter**
Fotolito *Colour separations* Reproduktion *Fotolitho's*	**FCM - Milano (Italy)**
Stampa *Printing* Druck *Druk*	**Streben Spa - Cernusco s. N. (Milano - Italy)**
Realizzazione *Editorial production* Herstellungskoordination *Redactie en samenstelling*	**SEP Editrice - Cernusco s. N. (Milano - Italy)**
ISBN	**88 - 87110 - 01 - 8**

Printed in Italy - Ottobre 1997

Si ringrazia
AUTOSPRINT
settimanale di automobilismo sportivo leader in Italia,
fonte inesauribile di molti
dati statistici ripresi per questo libro.

F1

BARCELONA

SPA-FRANCORCHAMPS

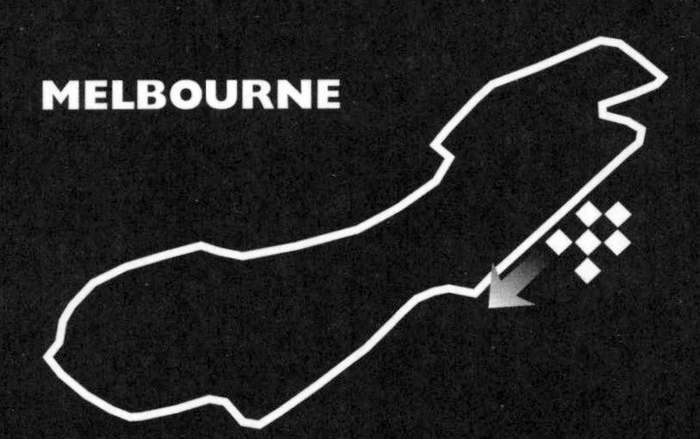
MELBOURNE

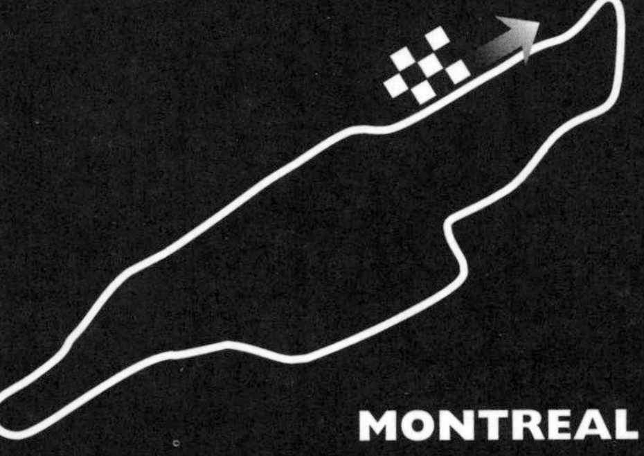
MONTREAL

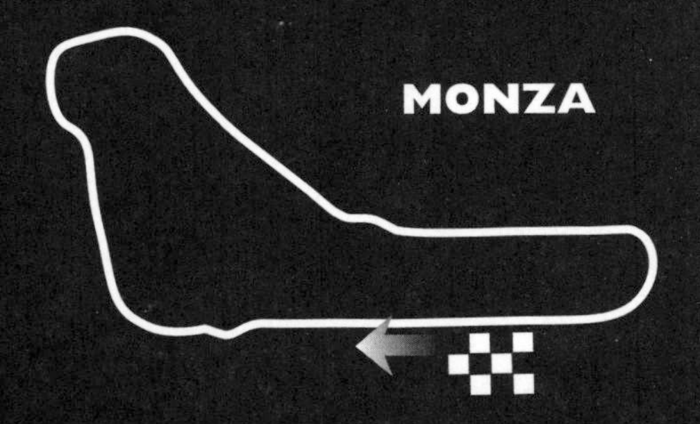
MONZA

INTERLAGOS

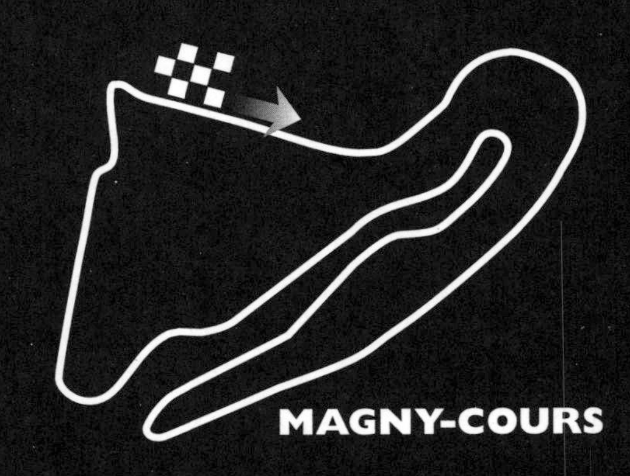
MAGNY-COURS

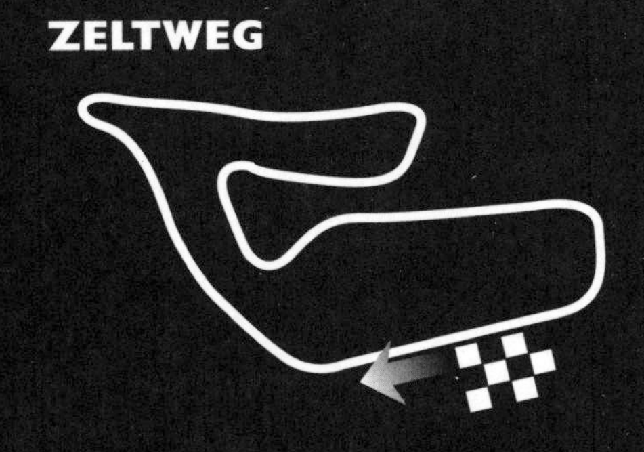
ZELTWEG

BUENOS
AIRES

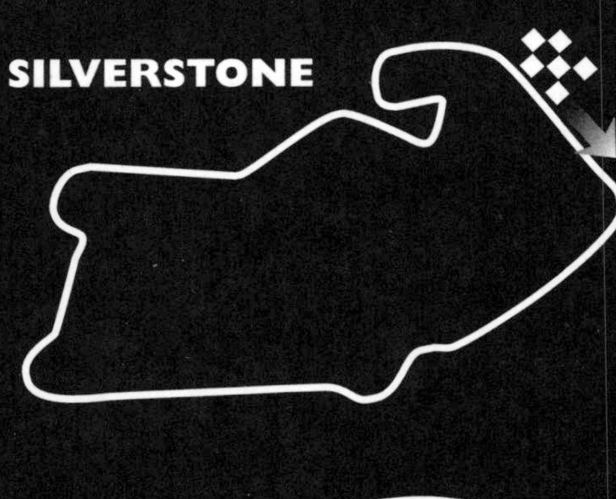
SILVERSTONE

NÜRBURGRING

IMOLA

HOCKENHEIM

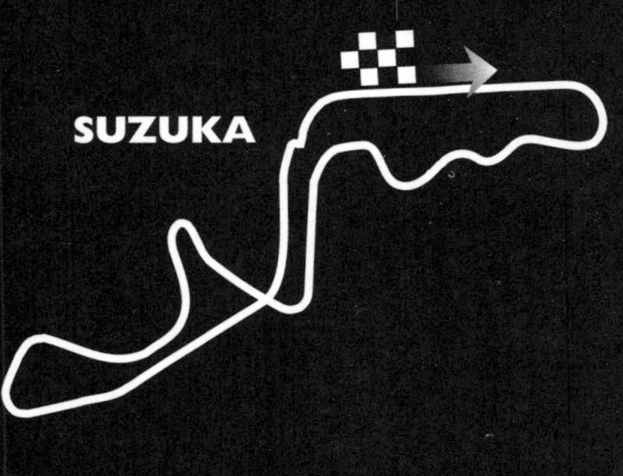
SUZUKA

MONTECARLO

HUNGARORING

JEREZ